TANTRA LEARNING FRAMEWORK

The Ego of I.D.
(instructional design)

Chaitanya Prabhu Hakkaladaddi

INDIA • SINGAPORE • MALAYSIA

ISBN 979-8-89277-841-1

Contents

Preface

Strange as it may seem, there are times when the obvious is not so obvious. Take, for instance, the connection between orange, the color, and orange – the fruit. I never made the connection when I was a kid, simply because all oranges came in shades of yellow.

The same goes for Turkey, the country, and turkey, the bird.

Similarly, though I practiced Tantra for over 30 years and have been an instructional designer for about 20 years, I didn't make any connection between the psychological system of the Tattvas and the many instructional design theories or models… until recently.

Tantra Learning Framework is a new instructional design methodology based on the 36 Tattvas of Kashmir Tantra. In developing this methodology, I have mapped the tattvas and the systems of tantric reality to traditional ID theories, models, and frameworks.

This parallelism is sometimes evident, but at other times, it's contrived, perhaps even implausible. Nevertheless, I have included those attempts to show that they don't work when we're trying to create meaningful learning content.

My strong interest in animal behavior has always motivated me to look beyond the work of B.F. Skinner: we need to go past operant conditioning to comprehend intelligent behavior. Also, I like to study humans as part of the animal kingdom and compare us to other animals.

While studying any behavior, it's essential to recognize that intelligence comes in many forms. Skinner's work does not fully capture the richness of cognition since many animals display problem-solving abilities, tool usage, metacognition, and language-like communication.

Whales even have what we usually classify as "culture." And human behavior can often manifest in complete disregard for consequences.

Studying humans within the broader animal kingdom can provide valuable insights into our nature and abilities. For example, comparing human and animal forms of intelligence may help identify the following:

- Universal traits that all intelligent systems share
- Components of intelligence that are uniquely human
- Evolutionary origins of higher cognitive functions

We must take a broad view of intelligence to develop effective learning frameworks, incorporating insights from ethology, primatology, cognitive science, and comparative psychology. Correctly understanding human intelligence requires studying our differences from animals and our continuities.

Overall, an interdisciplinary approach that combines the study of human learners with research on animal cognition and ancient psychological systems is likely to yield the most comprehensive and accurate learning models. I don't want to call these systems "spiritual" simply because the word spirituality – like religion – is quite sullied.

In this context, I've also had to draw parallels with traditional Western psychological systems to make the tattva hierarchy understandable.

While the tattvas represent ancient wisdom, translating that wisdom into modern psychological terms helps make it accessible to a broader audience. Jungian and Freudian psychology provide helpful analogies to which readers familiar with Western thought can relate. For example, one lower tattva, Prakriti, corresponds to Freud's Id (the primal, instinctual part of the mind). The middle tattvas map roughly onto Freud's Ego and Superego, representing rational thought and moral conscience.

The higher tattvas then move beyond the personal unconscious into the collective unconsciousness Jung wrote about. These parallels, though imperfect, help create a framework for understanding how the tattva hierarchy reflects the different levels of consciousness within the human psyche.

Another model is Maslow's Hierarchy of Needs, wherein the highest level is self-actualization. Maslow's hierarchy can also provide a valuable framework for understanding the tattva system. Just as Maslow posited that lower-level needs must be met before the higher needs can be fulfilled, the lower tattvas represent primal, foundational states of consciousness that must be mastered before progressing to the higher tattvas.

However, the tattva system also goes beyond Maslow by including even higher levels of realization and self-actualization. These reflect a shift in identity and perception where the individual self dissolves into an experience of oneness and unity with all existence.

The Tantra Learning Framework translates that underlined sentence: "*These reflect a shift in self-perception where the individual transcends the current state of ignorance into an experience of knowledge and skillful empowerment.*"

Hence, while Maslow's hierarchy provides a useful analogy, the full scope of the ancient tattva wisdom points to a transcendence beyond what modern Western psychology has traditionally envisioned as the highest potential of human nature. The tattvas reveal a multidimensional map for evolving human consciousness at physical and mental levels.

Self-actualization covers a vast range and depth of emotions… That's obvious! A man may actualize himself by owning a house or ruling a country. Indeed, self-actualization encompasses a vast spectrum of human experience. On a basic level, it can mean satisfying our material needs and desires, whether through acquiring possessions or achieving professional success. For others, self-actualization involves much more than that.

It involves developing our full potential by growing emotionally, creatively, spiritually, and intellectually. It means listening deeply to our inner voice and following our unique purpose in life. For some, self-actualization may come through artistic expression, spiritual practice, or building deep connections with others. There is no single path or formula – each person's journey is different.

The key is continually striving for growth and evolution within ourselves, challenging limiting beliefs and expanding our sense of what is possible. As we actualize more of our innate capacities and live in greater alignment with our values, we experience deeper fulfillment and a sense of meaning. The journey has no end, as there are always higher aspects of ourselves waiting to be realized and expressed. Self-actualization is a lifelong process of discovering and becoming. It brings us in touch with our inherent wisdom, compassion, and creativity and allows us to offer our complete, unique gifts to the world.

For all this to be achieved, we need e-learning, simulations, gamified learning objects, and immersive, experiential learning seminars in 5-star resorts! I don't mean that in jest. Seriously, we can't expect wisdom to come from a WBT!

In Kundalini Tantra, the tattvas act as milestones for enlightenment. Pursuing enlightenment is a tremendous vocation for those with the time and motivation. And I wish them luck achieving Buddhahood.

Meanwhile, lesser mortals can be happy with a quick and effective training program that helps them with their daily jobs. I'm sure most of us would be existentially satisfied if we had to complete our work with fewer mouse clicks.

These are the goals of the Tantra Learning Framework.

Chaitanya Prabhu Hakkaladaddi

Shillong, 18 January 2024

About the Author

Chaitanya Prabhu Hakkaladaddi was Editor & Publisher of Debonair magazine for seven years before entering the world of e-learning. Almost immediately, he came across Howard Gardner's Multiple Intelligences Theory in an online course from Harvard Graduate School of Education. This opened up many possibilities for him in the Instructional Design space, helping him co-develop the Story Based Learning (StoBL) methodology when he was with Tata Interactive Systems (now MPS Interactive Systems) and envision many innovative learning solutions when he moved to Cognizant.

Chaitanya has developed training programs for multinational companies, schools, universities, and international organizations ranging from Qantas and Royal Mail (UK) to Pfizer and AT&T to educational consortiums catering to US School Districts.

He was a Learning Consultant in the US for companies such as Procter & Gamble, General Electric, and Caterpillar. He was also on deputation to the United Nations (UNFPA) in New York.

For the last eight years, he has been creating immersive learning solutions for Multiple Intelligences Homeschool – an institution that fosters homeschooling, trains teachers in AI tools, and guides parents interested in genuine education. During this time, he has also been homeschooling his two daughters.

Chaitanya continues to write on the Science of Consciousness, Existentialism, Evolutionary Theories, and Tantra. He recently published *Tantra 2.0: Modern Interpretations of an Ancient Yoga*, in which he combines the Science of Consciousness with Tantra Yoga.

His other books are *Tantra Awakening: 8 Pathways to Enlightenment* and *12 Lesson Plans based on Multiple Intelligences Theory: The Narrative Entry Point Methodology*.

1

ONE: BRAIN

That is the number of brains a human has… unlike an Octopus with nine brains.

Humans and octopuses may differ in the number of brains they possess, but our cognitive abilities are equally fascinating. While an octopus has nine brains, each dedicated to controlling its eight tentacles and one to oversee its head, humans rely on a single, complex brain to navigate the world around us.

With its intricate network of neurons, the human brain is a marvel of evolution. It is responsible for our thoughts, emotions, and all the remarkable feats of intelligence that set us apart from other creatures. From solving complex mathematical equations to composing symphonies, the human brain can perform remarkable feats.

But what makes the human brain truly remarkable is its adaptability. Our brains continuously grow and change throughout our lives, forming new neuronal connections and pathways in response to our experiences. This phenomenon, known as neuroplasticity, allows us to learn, remember, and adapt to new situations.

Octopuses may have specialized brains for each tentacle, but their cognitive abilities differ. Octopuses are brilliant creatures, capable of solving puzzles, camouflaging themselves, and even opening jars. Their distributed nervous system, with brains in their tentacles, allows them to perform multiple tasks simultaneously.

Humans possess a unique blend of cognitive abilities, emotions, and social intelligence. Our brains enable us to communicate, empathize, and connect with others deeply. From forming lifelong friendships to building complex societies, our ability to collaborate and cooperate is deeply ingrained in our nature.

But sometimes we cannot open a jar!

Human Brain as a Serial Processor

While we may marvel at the octopus's nine brains, let's also consider another aspect of the human brain: it is a serial processor. It can handle only one task at a time, albeit quite rapidly, giving us the impression that it's handling things simultaneously.

However, the human brain remains a serial processor and can handle up to 3 tasks comfortably and rapidly. How does this affect learning?

First, the brain can only focus on and process one task or bit of information. We must focus on the task when learning new concepts or skills. Distractions can hamper our ability to encode data into long-term memory.

Second, the brain needs time to process and connect new information and prior knowledge. Rushing through information without sufficient reflection and integration does not allow for optimal learning. Taking breaks and spacing out study sessions over time helps strengthen memory.

Finally, the brain's limited processing capacity means that multitasking hinders learning. When we try to do two tasks simultaneously, our brain must switch back and forth between them. This switching comes at a cost to performance and retention for both functions.

A recent study showed how chatting and texting while studying diminishes learning while taking a break to send emails and browse the Net does not. It would augur well to delve deeper into this study. Did the chat have anything to do with the content being studied? Was the email about the subject matter at hand? Was the student browsing for free music downloads during his study break?

It's hard to determine what is a distraction and what isn't. Similarly, it's hard to tell when learning happens and what can hasten the process. But more about that later.

While the previous study provides some interesting insights, further research is needed to determine the precise effects of different distractions on learning. Some questions to consider are:

- What is the nature of the distraction? Casually checking social media is likely more detrimental than taking a brief break to make a call.

- How long does the distraction last? An occasional 5-minute break may aid concentration, while constantly checking notifications will disrupt focus.
- How engaging is the distraction? Highly stimulating distractions that fully capture our attention will impair learning more than passive distractions.
- What task are we trying to accomplish? Some distractions may be relevant and even helpful for specific goals.
- How does the individual learner respond? Some people can multi-task effectively, while others struggle to regain focus after interruptions.

The human brain's serial processing ability suggests that minimizing distractions and focusing entirely on the learning task will optimize information encoding and memory formation. However, periodic breaks and spacing out study sessions over time also benefit learning.

Box Jellyfish have no Brains

The fact that box jellyfish can learn from experience despite lacking a brain shows how complex and nuanced the concept of intelligence truly is.

Many animals demonstrate intelligence in ways that defy our traditional notions of what it means to be "smart." For instance, ants can navigate complex routes, termites can regulate temperatures in their colonies, and crows can craft and use tools.

Animal intelligence comes in many forms, and often in surprising places. While we think of intelligence as the province of large-brained mammals like ourselves, insects and other invertebrates demonstrate sophisticated cognitive abilities that challenge our notions of being "smart." The examples mentioned above are just a few of many:

- Bees perform an "orientation dance" to communicate the location of food sources to other hive members. This complex communication allows bees to locate and exploit diverse floral resources over a vast territory.

- Ant colonies coordinate tasks and respond to threats by exchanging chemical signals, demonstrating social intelligence at the group level.

- Octopuses are master escape artists, capable of puzzle-solving and problem-based learning. They can open child-resistant caps and unscrew jars to access food.

While we may never fully understand the nature of animal intelligence from our human perspective, these and many other examples show that cognitive complexity, adaptability, and problem-solving abilities are far more widespread in the living world than we may realize. Intelligence allows organisms to thrive in their environments and adapt to new challenges, though it takes many forms beyond what we typically recognize as "smart." Stepping back, this suggests that intelligence in the universe may be more abundant and diverse than we currently imagine.

This phenomenon is known as "non-human intelligence" and shows that intelligence comes in many forms beyond the conventional idea of a large brain capable of abstract reasoning.

The more we learn about animal cognition, the more we discover that intelligence is a spectrum, with humans at one end and other creatures demonstrating intelligence through behaviors that work for their particular needs and environments. This broader view of intelligence challenges us to rethink our place in the natural world and how we interact with the many unique life forms we share the planet with.

For a more in-depth and multi-sensory experience of this reality, I refer you to "An Immense World" by Ed Yong.

2

TWO: SEXES

That's the number of sexes humans have, male and female. While the third sex is a legal gender in India, it is not a metaphor that dominates our education. There are many differences in the brains of men and women, and they become pretty evident early in boys and girls.

The differences in male and female brains begin to emerge even before birth. Girls' brains tend to develop faster during the prenatal period, which gives them an advantage in language and fine motor skills at a young age.

After birth, boys' and girls' brains continue to develop along different trajectories. The corpus callosum, the bundle of nerve fibers connecting the two brain hemispheres, develops faster in girls. This may help explain why girls score higher than boys on verbal fluency and motor coordination tests during early childhood.

Meanwhile, parts of the brain involved in spatial processing and targeting of motor actions, like the parietal lobe and cerebellum, tend to develop earlier in boys. This could account for males' initial edge in targeting and spatial skills.

However, these differences are a matter of tendencies, not complex divisions. There is a wide variation in brain development among individuals of the same sex. Not all girls show the same brain patterns, and the same is valid for boys. Ultimately, environment and experience also shape how the brain wires throughout life.

For example, consider two ten-year-old children, John and Jane. From a young age, John has shown an aptitude for building things with blocks and Legos. He enjoys putting together jigsaw puzzles and figuring out how mechanical objects work. Jane, meanwhile, enjoys creative writing, making up stories, and reading books.

When tested for spatial and language skills at age 10, John performs above average on the spatial tasks, while Jane scores above average on the language assessments. This aligns with the typical differences in male and female brain development, with John's parietal lobe and related areas developing earlier to boost his spatial skills and Jane's corpus callosum giving her an advantage in language abilities.

However, there are many exceptions to this trend as well. Not all boys excel at spatial skills, and not all girls show advanced language development. Many factors beyond sex influence brain development, from genetics and environment to upbringing and personal interests. John and Jane's specific strengths likely also reflect the activities they were encouraged in and enjoyed the most from a young age.

Years ago, a school went to the local hospital in the US for an educational excursion. The girls were given the nurse's cap as a gift, and the boys were given the doctor's overcoat. The girls' parents were angry at this kind of discrimination.

The following year, on a similar trip, the same thing happened. The parents were furious. However, the parents were informed that children were asked to choose what they wanted. The girls chose the nurse's cap, and the boys chose the doctor's overcoat because all the doctors they saw were men, and all the nurses were women.

While stereotypes about gender differences in abilities are slowly changing, they still have a strong influence from a young age. The story of the children on the educational excursion shows how early gender biases can shape interests and perceived strengths.

However, children can develop skills and interests that transcend stereotypes with awareness and encouragement. Parents and educators play an essential role in exposing children to various activities, regardless of gender. For example, when a girl is interested in building things, her parents and teachers should nurture that curiosity rather than steer her toward more stereotypically "feminine" activities. The same applies to boys interested in creative writing or caring professions.

Children can be empowered to develop their strengths in all domains with conscious effort. Parents can expose children to counterexamples that challenge gender biases, such as female role models in STEM fields and male role models in caregiving professions.

It is clear that gender stereotypes form early and persist due to societal conditioning and lack of exposure to alternatives. While progress has been made, more needs to be done to nurture children's natural talents and interests regardless of gender. Children can develop a broader view of their potential with awareness and role models.

Educators play an essential role in shifting mindsets. Here are a few recommendations:

- Expose girls and boys to the same range of subjects and activities at school. Avoid 'pink-ifying' or 'blue-ifying' certain subjects.

- Have both female and male teachers and role models in all subjects. This helps break stereotypes about "gender-appropriate" roles.

- Implement gender-neutral policies that evaluate students based on their performance, not stereotypes.

- Provide positive examples of people in non-traditional gender roles as role models. Show that success has more to do with passion and talent than gender.

Parents can also make a difference:

- Avoid rigid gendering of toys and interests at home. Let children gravitate towards what interests them. (Give toy guns to girls!)

- Expose children to role models and examples of people in non-traditional gender roles.

- Praise children for their unique talents and interests, not for conforming to stereotypes.

These days, many girls aspire to careers in science, technology, engineering, and mathematics (STEM) fields that were traditionally male-dominated. Meanwhile, more boys are interested in creative arts, humanities, and caregiving roles.

This may be true because we now have scientists like Kalpana Kalahasti, who served as the deputy project director for the Chandrayaan-3 mission, and Ritu Karidhal Srivastava (also part of the Chandrayaan-3 mission) and is famously known as the "Rocket Woman of India."

But I grew up as a great fan of people like Jane Goodall, Dian Fossey, and Marie Curie. I wonder what kind of role models they had. Did their educational system encourage and motivate them to explore male-centric domains?

Today, even in girls' schools in India, the focus is on regimentation rather than catering to the unique learning needs of female students. The politically correct method has been to avoid making assumptions based on gender. This is fine, but I'm not discussing "prescribing" subjects based on gender. I am referring to the unique learning styles of girls and boys.

In all my years in the K-12 line of business, I don't remember anyone trying to customize learning around gender-specific learning styles.

Feminism and Science

> *"Is there a conflict between our commitment to feminism and our commitment to science? As both a feminist and a scientist, I am more familiar than I might wish with the nervousness and defensiveness that such a potential conflict evokes."*
>
> – Evelyn Fox Keller

Scientists have had some real challenges considering the types of issues that feminists have been raising. However, these challenges may end up being helpful in the long run. We've got to look at how feminist criticism of science has pointed out how male-dominated science has been and what that means for feminism.

This debate is necessary because it could help lead to a more accessible scientific research method. It might help scientists to listen to feminist criticism. Feminist ideas could even shine a light on parts of how science works (which may have gotten distorted over history) to keep the good things about science while making it more objective. But first, we need to review the different problems that feminists have brought up.

The criticisms feminists have made cover a wide range. They point out that science has had a clear male bias since men have led most scientific work. Keller states that the differences are like a spectrum that goes along with political feminism. Some problems are pretty easy to fix. But more radical views want significant, profound changes by looking at science's basic ideas and methods for signs of male bias.

However, sometimes people get all these ideas mixed up and think feminists want science not to be neutral anymore. Keller clarifies that how "male bias" is understood depends on how challenging it is, and even the most traditional scientists should be able to accept some of the less extreme views.

For example, in the liberal view, the complaint is about unfair job practices. This is based on the fact that almost all scientists are men. This criticism fits with traditional ideas of science and current liberal, equal rights politics. It's just a political issue that anyone who wants equal chances can agree on. With this view, having women around wouldn't change what science is.

> *Men decided what problems to solve, what inventions to invent, and what discoveries to make. If a woman had been resting under that tree when the apple suddenly hit her head, she probably would have figured out the gravity problem long ago.*

Has all humanity been held back by a "male science" and a long history of male inventions? This kind of criticism doesn't change our view of what science is or our belief that science is neutral. We might have ignored some specific problems, but we don't say science picks what to study – we know social forces have always played a role there.

For example, it's noted that all rat testing on learning has used male rats. While a simple reason given is that female rats have a four-day cycle that makes experiments harder, that doesn't answer the criticism. The assumption is that the male rat represents the whole species. There are plenty of similar examples in psychology.

In essence, we had to mug up all those theories, laws, and formulae in school because some Charlies – and not Charlenes – went about doing Science in a masculine way.

3

FIVE: SENSES

We have five senses: sight, hearing, smell, speech, and touch.

Our senses help us experience the world around us. They give us information about our surroundings and allow us to interact with our environment. Our sense of sight provides the most information, allowing us to perceive colors, shapes, movement, and space.

Our sense of hearing detects sounds that alert us to events. We rely on our hearing to communicate with others through speech. Our understanding of smell detects odors and aromas that trigger memories and emotions. Our sense of touch detects physical sensations like pressure, pain, heat, and cold. This sense also contributes to our awareness of our body and movement.

Together, our senses work to form a picture of the world. They help us navigate space, interact with objects and people, and experience pleasure and enjoyment. When one of our senses is impaired, it affects how we perceive and engage with our environment. We rely on our senses from the moment we are born and throughout our lives.

The Tattvas

At this point, it's imperative to introduce Tantra. Without describing the sunset, let me jump straight into it. Building on the previous discussion of the five senses, Tantra posits an expanded framework of "sensations" categorized as *tattvas*.

Rather than limiting senses to the conventional five associated with physical sense organs, Tantra considers any "entry point" or "pathway" through which we experience reality as a sense/experience. This includes sensations beyond the conventional ones.

Within the Tantric system, 36 tattvas – or categories of sensation – are identified, corresponding to the five commonly known senses. Meanwhile, the 10 Tattvas corresponding to the conventional five senses are as follows:

Levels 31 to 27: Odor, Flavor, Appearance, Touch, Sound

In Tantra, everything has these characteristics to a greater or lesser degree. Consider a menu item in a fancy restaurant: besides ensuring it tastes excellent, the chef puts considerable effort into making the plate look artistic. Where is the sound? It's in the ambient music!

This is an excellent example of understanding how the "tattva of the dish" does not "live" merely within the confines of the dish. Similarly, a tattva – any tattva – can manifest outside the confines of the space the object is occupying and outside of the one primary/striking attribute it possesses.

Levels 21 to 17: Nose, Tongue, Eyes, Skin, and Ears

The sense organs occupy another set of Levels in the Tantric Tattva System. They are our direct contact with reality. Each sense organ gives us a distinct sense of reality that may or may not be better! Dogs have about 200 to 300 million olfactory receptors compared to about 5 to 6 million human receptors.

The information we receive through our senses shapes our perception of reality. The various sense organs allow us to experience different aspects of reality, but each provides only a partial view. All sense perceptions are valid and valuable in their own right, and no single sense reveals the absolute truth (whatever "absolute truth" means to you).

The difference in olfactory receptors between humans and dogs is one example of how perception varies between species. While a dog's superior sense of smell allows it to experience certain aspects of reality more acutely, that does not necessarily mean their overall experience of reality is "better." It is simply different, shaped by the senses they possess.

Qualia

> *"The status of qualia is hotly debated in philosophy, largely because it is central to a proper understanding of the nature of consciousness. Qualia are at the very heart of the mind-body problem."*
>
> – Plato Project, Stanford University.

A quale (singular of qualia) is a person's subjective experience. It is an intrinsic sensation one feels, knows, and usually does not put into words. One may put it into words only to get a grasp of it because language provides us with words to "grasp" the meaning of something. In doing so, we "give" meaning to things but reduce our unique experiences to the lowest common denominator of a common language.

Describing Private Experiences in Social Constructs

If we had words for ourselves – a personal and private language – then there would be no problem. However, Ludwig Wittgenstein argued that private languages are impossible since language can only exist within a social context.

https://plato.stanford.edu/entries/private-language/

"The idea of a private language was made famous in philosophy by Ludwig Wittgenstein, who, in his book Philosophical Investigations, explained it thus: *The words of this language refer to what only the speaker can know – to his immediate private sensations. So, another person cannot understand the language.*

"This is not intended to cover (easily imaginable) cases of recording one's experiences in a personal code, for such a code, however obscure, could, in principle, be deciphered. Wittgenstein had in mind a language conceived as comprehensible only to its single originator because the things that define its vocabulary are necessarily inaccessible to others.

"Immediately after introducing the idea, Wittgenstein argues there cannot be such a language. The importance of drawing philosophers' attention to a largely unheard-of notion and then arguing that it is unrealizable lies in the fact that an unformulated reliance on the possibility of a private language is arguably essential to mainstream epistemology, philosophy of mind, and metaphysics from Descartes to versions of the representational theory of mind which became prominent in late twentieth-century cognitive science."

Therefore, qualia are often seen as a problem for materialist theories of mind since they seem fundamental to physical descriptions.

However, we can still gain valuable insights into qualia by investigating consciousness and subjective experience using the tools of science, philosophy, and first-person accounts. Studying qualia may help us better understand the relationship between mind and matter and how our perceptions shape our sense of reality.

While we may never fully grasp the ineffable essence of another person's qualia, honoring subjective experience as a valid source of truth can help enrich our collective understanding of the human condition.

Hence, Tantra provides us with techniques to communicate with ourselves using symbols and sounds that appeal to our inner cognitive workings. These techniques are designed to bypass the limitations of language and tap into the realm of qualia.

While words are a valuable tool for communicating specific ideas, they are an imperfect vessel for conveying the richness of inner experience. Tantra teaches that direct perception – unmediated by thoughts and language – can reveal a far more vast and wondrous reality.

Tantra also tells us that specific, ritualized actions can bypass the vulgar (commonplace, lacking sophistication) communication systems.

4

EIGHT: MULTIPLE INTELLIGENCES

Howard Gardner's Multiple Intelligences Theory proposes eight intelligences in human beings. Gardner started with seven intelligences but then added another. He hypothesized a ninth intelligence a few years ago.

Gardner's theory proposes that eight intelligences define the human ability to process information. These intelligences are:

1. Linguistic – Ability to understand and use language.
2. Logical-Mathematical – Ability to think logically and reason mathematically.
3. Spatial – Ability to visualize and work with spatial concepts.
4. Musical – Ability to understand and produce music.
5. Bodily-Kinesthetic – Ability to control one's body and handle objects skillfully.

6. Interpersonal – Ability to understand and interact with others.

7. Intrapersonal – Ability to understand oneself.

8. Naturalistic – Ability to recognize and understand patterns in nature.

1. Linguistic

Consider a young child who can speak in complete sentences by age two. This shows a high level of linguistic intelligence at an early age. The child can quickly grasp the rules of grammar and vocabulary and apply them to form new words and sentences. As the child grows, they may develop an early interest in reading books, writing stories, and engaging in conversations. With nurturing, this linguistic intelligence can help the child excel in language-related subjects like literature and writing as they progress through school.

2. Logical-Mathematical

A student who excels at math and logic puzzles from a young age also enjoys solving numerical and logical problems and spotting patterns and relationships between numbers and ideas. The student finds subjects like Algebra, Geometry, and Calculus easy to understand in school. They quickly grasp complex mathematical concepts and procedures and can solve problems methodically and logically. The student may also enjoy board and card games involving strategy, critical thinking, and deduction. With nurturing and proper education, this logical-mathematical intelligence can help the student pursue a career in STEM fields like mathematics, engineering, computer science, or data analysis.

3. **Spatial**

Consider an architecture student who excels at visualizing spatial concepts in 3 dimensions. They can easily imagine how buildings and structures will look from different angles and mentally rotate and manipulate objects in their mind's eye. In school, the student finds subjects like Geometry, engineering drawing, and 3D design intuitive and easy to grasp. They quickly develop skills in spatial visualization, mental folding, and mental rotation of objects. The student may also enjoy hobbies like Origami, jigsaw puzzles, and building with construction toys. With proper training and education, this spatial intelligence can help the student excel in architecture, engineering, interior design, or other visually spatial domains.

4. **Musical**

Children with this intelligence have an affinity for music from a young age. They enjoy listening to different types of music, singing along to songs, and playing musical instruments. They quickly develop rhythm, pitch, and tone skills through playing instruments or singing. The student may also enjoy composing their music and lyrics. With proper musical training and nurturing of this intelligence, the student could pursue a career in music performance, production, songwriting, or music therapy.

5. **Bodily-Kinesthetic**

A student who excels at sports and physical activities. They enjoy participating in team sports like basketball, soccer, and volleyball. The student moves with grace and coordination and has good hand-eye coordination. In school, the student quickly develops skills like throwing, catching, kicking, and hitting balls precisely. They also learn best through hands-on activities, experiments, and physical models. With proper nurturing and training, this bodily-kinesthetic intelligence could help the student pursue a career in sports, dance, physical therapy, and the like.

6. Interpersonal

A student who is very socially aware and attuned to the feelings of others. They enjoy interacting with their peers, listening to them, and helping them resolve their problems. In school, the student can form positive relationships with teachers and classmates and quickly resolve conflicts when they arise. The student has good communication and empathy skills and can effectively motivate and coordinate group efforts. They may enjoy participating in student government, organizing social events, or volunteering for community service projects. With training and development of this interpersonal intelligence, the student could pursue a career in teaching, counseling, human resources, event planning, or social work, where strong interpersonal skills are essential.

7. Intrapersonal

This student has a strong sense of self and knows their strengths, weaknesses, and preferences. They are self-motivated and self-directed, able to set meaningful goals for themselves. The student understands their emotions and feelings and can regulate their behavior accordingly. They can work independently in school and choose assignments that match their interests. With proper development of this intrapersonal intelligence, the student could pursue a career that matches their strengths and needs, where vital self-knowledge and self-management skills are essential.

8. Naturalistic

A student who shows early interest in nature and the outdoors. They enjoy observing and identifying plants, animals, weather patterns, and natural phenomena. In school, the student pays close attention to science lessons involving Biology, Ecology, and Earth Sciences. The student may easily recognize different species of birds, insects, and trees on the school grounds. With proper guidance and training, this naturalistic intelligence could help the student pursue a career in Environmental Science, Conservation, Botany, Zoology, or Wildlife Management, where understanding the natural world is essential.

The Ninth Intelligence: Existential Intelligence

Some students show an early interest in existential questions and philosophical thought. They ponder the meaning of life, the nature of reality, and humanity's place in the universe. The student enjoys Literature, History, and Social Studies lessons exploring these ideas in school and may spend free time reading Philosophy books. With proper guidance and exposure to different perspectives, this existential intelligence could help the student pursue a career that allows them to grapple with life's biggest questions and contribute to human wisdom and understanding. Careers that value existential intelligence include Philosophy, Theology, Metaphysics, Spirituality,

Futurism, and work that aims to improve the human condition through a more profound understanding of what it means to be human.

However, existential intelligence is not limited to certain professions – anyone can benefit from thinking deeply about the meaning and purpose of life.

The Impact

Gardner's theory has had a significant impact on education. It challenges the traditional view that intelligence is a single general ability and suggests that students have different cognitive strengths and weaknesses. This realization has led to more differentiated and personalized teaching methods that cater to students' varied intelligences.

The theory has also influenced our thoughts on creativity, talent, and genius. Rather than viewing these as manifestations of a single intelligence, Gardner's work suggests that individuals may excel in specific intelligence and domains.

For more information on his broader views of life, here is a link to one of his interviews:

https://www.howardgardner.com/howards-blog/interview-the-hidden-intelligences

5

NINE: EVENTS OF INSTRUCTION

Robert Gagne's Nine Events of Instruction provides a helpful framework for designing practical lessons aligned with learning outcomes. This has served us well, helping to align each screen (in an e-learning program) or a set of screens to a learning event.

As an extension of John Keller's ARCS Model (Attention, Relevance, Confidence, Satisfaction), Gagne's Events also helped e-learning developers add more screens in a WBT, increasing the cost.

(For more on the ARCS Model, refer to:

https://sphweb.bumc.bu.edu/otlt/teachingLibrary/Learning%20Theory/ARCSintegrated_handout.pdf)

Gagne's Nine Events of Instruction are as follows:

1. Gain Attention – Capture the learner's attention and interest before starting any instruction. This event primes the learners

and motivates them to pay attention to the upcoming content. There are various ways to gain a learner's attention:

Novelty: Using something novel, surprising, or unexpected at the start can grab the learner's attention. For example, I show an attractive video clip or image to set the context.

Relevance: Explaining how the upcoming content is relevant to the learner's goals and interests can motivate them to pay attention. Making real-world connections helps gain relevance.

Inquiry: Starting with an intriguing question or puzzle related to the topic can pique learners' curiosity and interest them in the following content. This works well for active learners.

Gaining attention at the very start sets the tone for effective learning. Learners who are attentive from the beginning are more likely to engage with and understand the rest of the instructional content. So, capturing the learner's interest and focus through novelty, relevance, or inquiry can improve learning outcomes later.

2. Inform Learners of Objectives – Clearly state what learners can do after the lesson. For example, Inform Learners of Objectives can be achieved by briefly summarizing the lesson at the start. Students can be told:

   "By the end of this lesson, you will be able to identify the main parts of a plant cell and explain the function of each part."

   How often have we corrected the sentence, "At the end of this lesson…" in our storyboards? However, does learning take place at the ninth Event? When we write, "By the end of this lesson…," should we also add, "hopefully?"

3. Stimulate Recall of Prior Learning – Activate relevant background knowledge to set the stage for new information.

   For instance, to stimulate recall of prior learning, an instructor could ask students to think of a plant they are familiar with and describe its parts. The instructor could then show an image of a plant cell and ask students to relate the parts of the plant cell to the plant they described earlier.

   As an illustration, imagine a Biology teacher who wants to teach students about plant cells. Before jumping into the details of each plant cell part, the teacher could say: "Raise your hand if you have a plant at home. What kind of plant do you have?" After a few students describe their plants, the teacher could say:

   "Those are all great examples of plants we are familiar with. Look closer inside a plant cell to see how it functions."

   The teacher could then show an image of a plant cell and relate each part to the parts of the plants the students described earlier, connecting new information to their prior knowledge of plants.

4. Present the Content – Explain the new material using examples, demonstrations, lectures, and other methods. Here, the instructor could show an image of a plant cell and label each part while explaining its structure and function. The instructor could say: "This outer boundary is the cell wall made of cellulose. It gives the plant cell its shape and protection.

Inside the cell wall is the cell membrane, which acts as a selective filter, controlling what enters and leaves the cell."

The instructor could then move to the following structure and explain: "These structures suspended in the fluid inside the cell are organelles called chloroplasts. Chloroplasts contain chlorophyll, which captures the energy from sunlight that the plant cell needs."

5. Provide Learning Guidance – Offer guidance, cues, and prompts to help learners organize and comprehend the information.

During a lesson on Parts of Speech, the teacher may provide cues to help students identify nouns. She may underline nouns in sample sentences as she reads them aloud or highlight them in a different color on slides. The teacher can also provide prompts like, "What is acting as a noun in this sentence?" and remind students of the definition of a noun. By guiding students through cues, prompts, and reminders, the teacher helps them organize and understand the new information about parts of speech.

As an illustration, imagine teaching students about fractions. To provide learning guidance, you could show visual representations of fractions using shapes divided into parts. You could provide prompts like, "Which parts represent the numerator? Which parts represent the denominator?" You could remind students of key terms like numerator, denominator, and proper fraction. These guidance techniques help scaffold students' understanding of fractions as they learn the new material.

6. Elicit Performance – Give learners opportunities to practice and apply their new knowledge and skills.

   For example, imagine you are teaching students about fractions. You could give students practice worksheets with fraction problems of varying difficulty to elicit performance from the students. You could start with simple tasks like identifying the numerator and denominator in given fractions and progress to more complex functions like adding, subtracting, multiplying, and dividing fractions.

   As the students work through the practice problems, you circulate the room and check their work. You provide feedback to correct mistakes and misunderstandings. You also ask the students to explain their reasoning and problem-solving process. This gives you insight into how well they apply the concepts to solve new problems.

   By providing multiple practice opportunities and checking in individually, you elicit students' performance and application of the new fraction skills.

7. Provide Informative Feedback – Provide feedback on learners' performance to clarify mistakes and misconceptions.

   For instance, imagine a student has just completed a worksheet on adding and subtracting fractions. You review their work and notice they made a mistake by adding the denominators instead of finding a common denominator first.

   You could say something like: "I see that you added the denominators when adding these fractions. However, to add fractions with different denominators, we first need to find a common denominator and then add the numerators. Let's try working through this problem together, step by step."

You then model the correct process of finding the common denominator and adding the numerators while explaining your thinking out loud. After providing this informative feedback on their mistake, you ask the student to try another similar problem on their own while you observe. You provide more targeted guidance and clarification if they repeat the same mistake.

By catching the misconceptions early and providing clear, step-by-step feedback, you give them the information they need to self-correct and apply the proper procedure for adding fractions with unlike denominators in the future.

8. Assess Performance – Evaluate learners' performance to determine if objectives were met.

After teaching a lesson on calculating the area of triangles, you give students a worksheet with ten practice problems. As you circulate the room and check their work, several students incorrectly add the lengths of two sides instead of multiplying base times height.

You call one of these students to the board to present their work. You say: "I see you added the two sides instead of multiplying base times height. The area formula for triangles is base times height divided by 2. Let's try working through this problem together, step by step."

You model finding the base and height on the diagram, then multiplying those values and dividing by 2. As you explain each step, you ask the student questions to check their understanding. After completing the example problem together, you ask the student to try another similar situation while you observe. If they make the same mistake again, you provide more clarification and targeted guidance until they can accurately calculate the area of a triangle.

9. Enhance Retention and Transfer – Provide activities to help learners remember and apply what they learned to new situations.

For example, after teaching a lesson on ratios and proportions, you assign students a project to find real-world examples of ratios and proportions in action. Students are tasked with taking photos of ratios and proportions they encounter daily and explaining the math concept illustrated.

Some students may photograph things like:

- Recipe instructions, which use ratios to proportion ingredients
- Maps, which use a proportion to scale distances
- Architectural plans, which use proportions of different measurements

Students then share their examples with the class in a gallery walk, explaining the ratio or proportion illustrated in their photo and how it applies to a concept from the lesson. Gagne's Nine Events of Instruction provides a systematic approach to designing effective instruction that supports different learning outcomes. The framework emphasizes vital components that activate learners' prior knowledge, present new information meaningfully, provide guidance and feedback, and assess learning. The nine events also recognize the need to accommodate individual differences among learners.

6

ORANGE IS NOT ORANGE

- According to Wikipedia, learning is acquiring new knowledge, understanding, behaviors, skills, values, attitudes, and preferences. It can also be defined as a process that leads to change due to experience.
- According to StatPearls, learning is the change in an organism's behavior resulting from prior experience. Learning theory explains how individuals acquire, process, retain, and recall knowledge during learning.
- According to Studycat, the Science of Learning describes learning as constructing new knowledge based on context and experience.
- According to Open Text WSU, there are three main types of learning: classical conditioning, operant conditioning, and observational learning.

- According to Quora, scientific learning fosters critical thinking skills. It encourages us to ask questions, seek evidence, evaluate information, and think analytically.

According to Pink Floyd, "We don't need no education."

There are many definitions of learning, and I'm not offering any new definitions or descriptions. I'm merely focusing on those aspects of learning that help create connections between ideas and concepts. These connections could be simplistic, or they could be highly symbolic and abstract.

Indeed, we already know that we learn every day. We collect something new, even acquiring the tiniest bit of information. Watching the news is one prominent learning event – even the couch potato learns something new because he's browsing numerous channels.

Learning occurs through connections and associations that form webs of meaning and understanding. New ideas and information attach themselves to this web, strengthening some connections while weakening others. When we learn effectively, we form connections that give us many ways to retrieve and apply what we've learned.

I was about 21 years old, in the last year of college, when it suddenly struck me that I had never associated the color orange with the fruit orange. How does one miss such an obvious connection? Perhaps because no orange (sweet lime, tangerine, or lemon) is orange? They are all some shade of yellow.

A similar gap in my learning occurred when I realized that the bird turkey and the country Turkey are named the same. I guess the Turks too realized it – after all these years – and changed their name to Turkiye.

Learning is a process wherein neuronal connections are made. Recall the structure of the neuron with the axon and the dendrites. The structure and connections between neurons form the basis of learning and memory. Within each neuron, electrical signals travel along the axon toward the dendrites of other neurons, causing them to fire. When neurons fire together repeatedly, connections between them are strengthened. These connections form pathways that encode memories and knowledge.

This process of neural connections is known as long-term potentiation. The more a pathway is activated, the stronger it becomes, making retrieval and use of that knowledge faster and easier. Conversely, connections that are rarely used become weakened over time.

The axons and dendrites allow neurons to form intricate networks in the brain, serving as the biological substrate for all forms of learning. By forging new links and strengthening old ones, we continue acquiring knowledge and building upon what we already know.

Pavlov's Dogs

Learning also involves making connections between seemingly unrelated concepts. When Ivan Pavlov trained his dogs to salivate on hearing a bell, he invented (discovered?) "Conditioning."

Pavlov's classical conditioning experiments demonstrated how learning occurs by forming associations between stimuli and responses. By repeatedly pairing a neutral stimulus like a bell with a reflexive stimulus like food, Pavlov conditioned the dogs to associate the sound of the bell with the arrival of food. Over time, the bell triggered the salivation response, showing that the dogs had formed a mental association between the two stimuli.

Classical conditioning is a simple form of learning that underlies more complex cognitive processes. The primary mechanism – where a neutral stimulus becomes associated with an inherent response through repeated exposure – helps explain how we form associations that influence our behavior and decision-making. Our emotional responses and preferences are shaped by conditioning that occurs without conscious awareness.

So, while Pavlov's discovery may seem trivial, his experiments shed light on fundamental principles about how the mind forms connections between different experiences. The concept of conditioning has profoundly influenced Psychology, helping us understand how we acquire likes and dislikes, fears, and passions. It shows how much of our knowledge is learned by gradually forging links between seemingly unrelated events.

These "aha moments" of insight can lead to significant leaps in understanding. Sometimes, learning happens suddenly when a new concept instantly clicks into place. Other times, it is a gradual process of making small connections that accumulate over time.

The human brain is wired to make associations. Our neurons form networks of connections that link related ideas and experiences. When we learn something new, our brain connects that information to what we already know. This helps us understand and remember the new concept.

Making connections through analogies and metaphors can be particularly powerful for learning. Comparing a new idea to something familiar helps translate the new concept into terms we already grasp. Even simple word associations can aid memory and understanding. Learning through making connections also means recognizing gaps in our knowledge and seeking to fill those gaps. They motivated me to make the neuronal connections I was missing.

Tantra Learning Framework proposes articulating and prescribing how these connections should be made across and beyond each level.

In this context, the Allen Institute is on a mission to create an Atlas of the Brain to uncover how its circuits generate thought, perception, and action. The project aims to document where every gene is active in the brain to create an atlas of gene expression across different regions and cell types. This brain atlas will provide a foundational map of the molecular anatomy of the brain, revealing important insights into how the brain functions at a cellular and molecular level.

By mapping the activity of genes throughout the brain, researchers hope to gain a more comprehensive understanding of how neurons form circuits, communicate, and give rise to behaviors and cognition. This brain atlas could also help identify genes involved in neurological disorders and pave the way for more targeted treatments.

The Allen Institute's ambitious effort reflects the complexity of the human brain, with its nearly 100 billion neurons and 100 trillion connections. Mapping gene activity across this vast neural network requires analyzing gene expression in thousands of tiny brain subregions.

Once complete, the Allen Brain Atlas promises to be a powerful resource for neuroscientists, providing a molecular framework for exploring some of the most profound questions about the human mind. Revealing the genetic underpinnings of neural circuits could fuel discoveries about the biological basis of perception, memory, decision-making, and many other cognitive processes. The more we can understand how the brain gives rise to thought and intelligence, the closer we come to realizing the full potential of the human mind.

When we maximize these connections through reasoning, analogies, associations, and seeking to fill gaps in our knowledge, our learning becomes more profound and longer-lasting. The more connections we make, the more we learn.

To maximize learning, we should actively seek connections between new ideas and what we already know. We should look for patterns and relationships, form mental images and analogies, and find real-world applications. Asking questions about how new information relates to our interests and experiences helps cement those connections meaningfully.

Making mistakes and correcting misconceptions also helps us learn by highlighting gaps in our understanding. Testing our knowledge through practice and application strengthens the connections we form. Discussing new ideas with others exposes us to different perspectives that create more complex webs of understanding.

Conditioning through Indoctrination

The late educational philosopher Kieran Egan observed that we use the term indoctrination whenever children are taught ideas, beliefs, and values that conflict with our own. It's a pattern with a long history, reaching back to the emergence of "common schools" in the 1840s.

While indoctrination has negative connotations, teaching children values and ideas is essential to their education and upbringing. The key is teaching children how to think critically and exposing them to multiple perspectives, allowing them to decide. Students should have the tools to evaluate information and form reasoned opinions.

Rather than avoiding "indoctrination" altogether, a more constructive approach is to be transparent about our values while exposing children to multiple viewpoints. We should emphasize that many reasonable people disagree on complex issues and demonstrate how responsible citizens navigate such differences respectfully. The ultimate antidote to indoctrination is an education that nurtures independence of thought and spirit.

7

TANTRA

Tantra is not a Philosophy; it is a technique. It is not a belief system, religion, or doctrine. It is a technique. It does not prescribe love, hate, or indifference: it is technique… techniques that one may use for Good or Evil.

When Tantra reveals itself through yogic asanas, it does so through experiences unique to each individual. Most of these experiences are explainable through a common language, but many are not. Cognitively, these experiences are novel, arising from an altered consciousness, involving unusual sensations and uncommon manifestations.

What is Tantra?

Tantra is one of the many spiritual traditions of ancient India, which influenced Hinduism and Buddhism. It comprises many diverse traditions, and each tantric practice has the awakening of consciousness or achieving enlightenment at its core.

The term is conjured from two Sanskrit words, *Tanoti* and *Trayate,* where *Tanoti* means "to expand" and *Trayate* means "to liberate." It also owes its meaning to the parts of the word "Tantra," wherein "tan" means the body and "tra" means mechanism or tool. This implies that tantriks use the body as a tool for liberation.

In the dualistic sense, the body is expanding to liberate the mind. This interpretation also works, but the ultimate aim of Tantra is to achieve oneness with reality or to become inseparable from the expanse of universal consciousness. Tantra destroys this mind-body duality and body-environment, bringing about a communion of the creature with the cosmos.

What Tantra is Not!

Tantra does not mean "to weave" and has nothing to do with the weaving loom. This is a literal – and entirely incorrect – translation by non-Sanskrit, Western experts. For more details, refer to *Tantra Illuminated* by Christopher Wallis (https://hareesh.org).

A Bit of History

Tantra is at least 2500 years old. The word Tantra was first found in the Rig Veda, which is now about 3500 years old. Patanjali mentions Tantra, which forms the basis of Buddhism (about 2500 years old). As it grew, practices changed, concepts transformed, and new meanings arose. Hence, there is no absolute, authoritative source of Tantra. In this context, why bother beyond a point?

The more meaningful and satisfying aspects of Tantra are in its daily practice. Therefore, do not be caught up in academic nit-picking. Tantra Yoga offers an entire philosophy (because Yoga loosely translates as Philosophy) by combining teachings from the ancient Indian Schools of Thought (*Nyaya*, *Vaisheshika*, *Samkhya*, *Yoga*, *Mimamsa*, and *Vedanta*). When these combinations differed, they gave rise to different traditions, and one of these traditional systems is the Non-Dual Shaiva Tantra (NST) philosophy.

My earlier book, "Tantra 2.0: Modern Interpretations of an Ancient Yoga," draws upon Non-Dual Shaiva Tantra (NST) Philosophy's interpretations and executions of daily practices. NST is also known as Kashmir Tantra. This is the only tradition of Tantra that I have found meaningful from a scientific perspective and appealed to my modern sense of existence.

The 36 Tattvas

What exactly is a tattva? The word "tattva" doesn't directly translate to one English word. At its most basic, a tattva can be considered a thing, quality, or intelligence. But it's more than just one of those – a tattva combines all three into a unified reality experience.

Traditional yoga first proposed the idea of tattvas. However, Shaiva Tantra Yoga expanded on this to introduce additional tattvas, bringing the total number to 36. These 36 Tattvas are described as different levels of reality.

Within Shaiva Tantra, the idea of being external is an illusion. But breaking the tattvas down individually helps us to understand them better. Hence, the lower tattvas represent more superficial or apparent levels of reality, while the higher tattvas signify deeper, more profound levels of understanding. Here is a breakdown of Shaivism's 36 Tattvas, listed from most superficial to most profound.

Levels 36 to 32: Earth, Water, Fire, Wind, Space

The Natural Tattvas

The first five tattvas correspond to the essential elements of nature – superficial reality. But it's inaccurate to think of one component, like Earth, as "lower" or less important than another, like Wind or Fire. You also can't separate these elements from their defining characteristics – for example, the forcefulness and breeziness of Wind.

For example, consider how Earth is the foundation for all life. Earth's soil, landforms, and geology provide the physical structure and nutrients that plants need to grow. Plants then serve as food and shelter for animals. Earth's gravity and magnetic field also shape the environment of living things.

Water is another fundamental element that's essential for life. Around 70% of the human body is water; virtually all living organisms require water to survive. Water acts as a solvent, carrying nutrients into cells and waste products out of cells. Water regulates body temperature and acts as a lubricant and cushion for joints. Without water, life as we know it could not exist.

While often associated with destruction, fire also plays a vital role in nature. Fire recycles nutrients, releasing them back into the environment. It helps regenerate ecosystems by clearing dead plant material and opening cones and seeds.

Wind serves the crucial function of dispersing seeds and spores, which allows plants to colonize new habitats. Wind also helps regulate the planet's temperature by distributing heat from the equator to the poles. Many animals, like birds, have also evolved to use wind currents for migration.

Moreover, these elements don't indeed exist independently of each other. Each occupies and is contained within Space. Space itself exists within every atom. They are intertwined in varying combinations.

Levels 31 to Level 27: Odor, Flavor, Appearance, Touch, Sound

The Sense Tattvas – The First Set

Through these tattvas, our senses interact with the world. In Tantra, everything has qualities like odor, flavor, appearance, touch, and sound to different degrees.

The sense of sound also has a significant impact on education. Hearing the teacher's voice and instructions helps students focus and stay engaged. Background sounds and noises in a classroom can distract students and negatively impact their learning. Indeed, music has also boosted students' concentration and mood while studying, but it depends on the kind of music you listen to.

For example, playing classical music during study hall or while doing homework can improve students' concentration and productivity. Meanwhile, noisy environments make it more complicated for students to comprehend what they are reading or being taught. How a teacher speaks and modulates their voice also influences how well students understand and retain the information being taught. Using a calm, clear tone of voice and speaking appropriately provides scaffolding to help students follow along and comprehend complex ideas and explanations.

Combining background music, quiet, focused students, and visually engaging teaching methods creates a practical learning experience. The sounds, sights, and explanations work together to enhance students' understanding of the concepts and immerse them fully in the lesson. The teacher has to put a lot of thought into how all the senses – including sound – could be optimized to improve the students' learning and enjoyment.

As another example, consider a walk through a park on a sunny day. The sights and sounds of the park – the trees, grass, and other people – form the basis of the experience. But the feelings it evokes within you and your thoughts while walking also contribute significantly. Your whole sensory and mental state at that moment combines to create the experience of that walk, not just the physical space you occupy.

Levels 26 to 22: Intestines, Genitals, Feet, Hands, Mouth

Organic Tattvas

These tattvas are apparent. Our intestines help expel waste from our bodies, an important function we don't have direct control over. Our genitals are used for reproduction, another process controlled by our autonomic nervous system rather than our conscious minds. Our feet enable us to get around from place to place through locomotion. Our hands let us hold and interact with things around us. This allows us to experience something by touching it and understanding its properties. We can only understand an object when we pick it up and feel it ourselves.

Our mouths let us chew food for digestion and talk with others. We have direct control over our hands, feet, and speech. However, specific internal processes like digestion and reproduction are managed automatically rather than consciously.

It's fascinating how our bodies give us different tools for experiencing and navigating the world through voluntary and involuntary systems. Each part plays a vital role in keeping us alive and able to interact with our surroundings.

Levels 21 to 17: Sight, Smell, Taste, Touch, Hearing

Animal Tattvas, Also the Second Set of the Sense Tattvas

Our fantastic sense organs connect us to the world. We all know the basic five senses, but we often restrict our understanding to experiences only through these senses.

It's interesting how each animal might experience reality differently than us. It shows that what we consider "reality" through our senses is unique to our experience. An animal may perceive things differently. Even slight differences in our bodies can lead to different realities.

Levels 16 to 12: Mind, Ego, Intelligence, Instinct, Consciousness

The Human Tattvas

It is essential to mention that Yoga – besides the practice of physical exercises – also includes training the mind. Specific asanas (yogic postures or poses) in many Yoga Schools enhance particular attitudes.

One yoga asana may teach us humility, while another yoga posture may teach us devotion.

16. Mind

This is one's ability to pay attention. Focusing your mind, paying attention, concentrating on a task, etc., is at the level of the mind. Recall the ARCS Model and Gagne's Events of Learning: This unique feature of higher-order animals has evolved to achieve evolutionary success.

When students learn new concepts in school, they must focus on what the teacher says and the material covered. Any distractions or stray thoughts can hinder the learning process. For example, if a teacher is giving a history lecture and explaining a vital event, the students who can concentrate fully and block out distractions will gain a better understanding and retain more information than those who let their minds wander. Therefore, developing good concentration skills through practice is an integral part of the learning process for students.

15. Ego

This is one's ability to create an idea of the Self and form an image of the Self (a picture of one's personality). I create the impression of Myself! However, the Ego diminishes as we grow older. Unlike most people, a self-centered person has a small ego, so they behave in a manner wherein they have to protect what little they have.

In contrast, a child has a massive ego because it possesses everything it sees or perceives. Everything is within the sphere of its being! The infant has no sense of material possession, so its consciousness is posited in every object or creature it perceives. A doll or a warm blanket is as living as a parent is. A pet cat or dog is identical to itself.

However, as the infant grows, its experiences limit and constrain the Self. Fire is painful, a beetle is bitter, and mud is distasteful… these unpleasant experiences are imprinted and lead the child to form the notion of "Not Me" or a "painful/unpleasant" thing. Adding to the "Not Me" list, the idea of "Me" gets refined and limited.

In the modern world – especially in Western, industrialized societies – ego often creates the most significant barrier to self-realization.

Granthis: The Obstacles to Awakening/Learning

In my book, "Tantra Awakening: 8 Pathways to Enlightenment," I briefly speak about Granthis. The Sanskrit word Granthi means knot or doubt. These knots bind us… They are psychological barriers to liberation (Moksha) and prevent prana from its path along Sushumna Nadi.

Let's replace "awakening" and "liberation" with "learning," and we immediately see how this complex psychological system creates barriers to internalizing knowledge.

The three Granthis are:

1. Brahma Granthi functions near Muladhara Chakra, which signifies attachment to materialism and pursuit of vulgar pleasures. It represents laziness and other Tamasic qualities.

   Being lazy about learning is an attitude created over many years, and I have not come across any research elaborating on its causes. I am enthusiastic about learning Zoology, but I shut off regarding Botany.

2. Vishnu Granthi operates near Anahata Chakra and represents excessive emotional attachment. It represents Rajasic qualities such as ambition and domination.

   This granthi is about having a pet subject or a favorite concept/ intellectual belief/hypothesis that we can't tolerate being questioned, let alone destroyed.

   I love Darwinism, so I would hate to come across any evidence that supports or proves the notion of Intelligent Design.

3. Rudra Granthi functions near Ajna Chakra. (Rudra is another name for Shiva.) It is associated with egoism and egotism. It is over-identification with the super-ego.

   Perhaps the most powerful of the Granthis is an absolute denial of anything that challenges one's existential beliefs. Having fashioned one's identity around a set of beliefs and lived life by those beliefs, it's hard to accept them being crushed.

These Granthis have the names of the Hindu Trinity to show how powerful they can be to surmount.

To what extent do these barriers block and even turn off learning? Tantra Learning Framework will ask these questions equivalent to the Training Needs Analysis phase.

14. Intelligence

Our popular understanding of "intelligence" – when the "Me" starts separating from the "Not Me," using reasoning. This mental mechanism creates the distinction by enabling differentiation between things.

For instance, imagine you are explaining the role of intelligence in distinguishing the self from others to a group of college students. You define intelligence as the mental ability that enables a person to learn, reason, and think abstractly. You point out that infants begin distinguishing between themselves and the objects around them as they develop. Intelligence helps form this distinction by enabling logical reasoning and abstract thought.

You give the example of a toddler learning that the stuffed animal is not alive like they are. Through observation and reasoning, the child understands that the toy cannot think or feel like a natural person.

As the students grow, intelligence continues to refine their sense of self, enabling them to understand more complex ideas. They learn about emotions, personalities, skills, and interests that make them unique individuals. Intelligence helps them see how they are both similar to and different from others. It gives them the mental tools to think logically about abstract concepts like the self, identity, and personality.

You conclude by emphasizing that intelligence is just one aspect of human nature, and other factors like emotion, relationships, and experiences also shape a person's sense of self. Intelligence plays a vital role in enabling humans to develop abstract reasoning and conceptual thought, allowing us to define and understand the complex concept of the self.

Thanks to Howard Gardner, we know of 8 (even 9) distinct intelligences, each having origins in the brain.

Once again, Tantra Learning Framework explores how all instructional material becomes intelligence only after it has been assimilated or internalized. This implies a non-separation or a non-duality from the learning material. Till that happens, all ingested learning material must be considered undigested food that may be expelled through excretion.

13. Instinct

Instincts manifest themselves – we don't need to create learning around them. We also don't need to factor them in the context of modern education: it will be enough to know that they exist and that they shouldn't be ignored.

12. Consciousness of Self

In most Yoga Systems, this is the highest form of "experience," but not in Shaiva Tantra. A simple form of Tantra meditation will reveal the many diverse manifestations of this tattva. The consciousness of Self is comparable to the super-ego, and it's the framework within which all the tattvas mentioned above exist.

This tattva symbolizes a level of attainment. This is where it all begins for the sake of the Tantra Learning Framework. To develop learning material, this is the entirety of the Learner Needs Analysis.

Levels 11 to 7: Cause and Effect, Time, Desire, Knowledge, Action

The Intellectual Tattvas

Tantra Learning Framework is posited in the Intellectual Tattvas, also called the Veils of Ignorance. The idea is that learning (enlightenment/liberation) occurs when these veils are lifted. These tattvas are covered in detail in the chapter titled Tantra Learning Framework.

8

THE EGO OF I.D.

I was in a requirements gathering discussion with the training manager of a multinational bank some years ago. She wanted a plain WBT of about 60 minutes. I proposed a simulation at the start, but she said she didn't want one: "… a plain vanilla page-turner will work just fine," she said.

After 45 minutes of detailed instructions and articulating the learning goals of the training program, I said, "A simulation will be the right fit for these requirements."

"Have you ever heard a single word I've said," she uttered in exasperation.

The following text is what Hypotenuse generated:

I paused for a moment, reflecting on her frustration. While simulations can be highly effective learning tools, I needed to understand her reservations better.

"I understand your preference for a simple page-turner," I said. "Before we decide on the final design, could you help me understand the rationale behind your aversion to simulations? There may be important considerations I'm not aware of."

She sighed. "It's not that simulations can't be useful. But in the past, they've caused delays and cost overruns. My managers want this training deployed quickly and on a tight budget."

"That's a fair point," I replied. "A well-designed simulation can provide great value, but poorly executed ones can cause problems. Perhaps we could discuss creating a simple, focused simulation that aligns with your goals for timeliness and budget."

She considered this for a moment. "Alright, let's talk through some options then."

We began to brainstorm simulation ideas that would engage learners while staying within the constraints she faced. By keeping an open mind and a collaborative spirit, we ultimately found a simulation approach we both felt good about.

That is not what happened.

I remonstrated that I had indeed heard what she had been saying (a single word!), and we went on for the next 5 minutes to finalize timelines.

The Tantra Learning Framework understands that training initiatives must ultimately serve organizational goals and budgetary constraints. While simulations and other engaging elements can enhance learning, they must be implemented pragmatically with an eye toward costs and timelines.

Communicating openly with clients allows us to find creative solutions that maximize value within their parameters. Rather than insist on our preferred instructional methods, we strive to collaborate and determine what approach will provide the most significant benefit given real-world business realities.

This means acknowledging budget ceilings and time pressures as legitimate considerations, not excuses to compromise quality. Within those boundaries, we can often identify opportunities to improve impact and ROI through focused innovations. But we do so with transparency and a spirit of partnership, earning clients' trust through meaningful results that meet or exceed their expectations.

9

LEARNING FRAMEWORKS

Teaching and learning frameworks are research-informed models for course design that help instructors align learning goals with classroom activities, create motivating and inclusive environments, and integrate assessment into learning. Frameworks like Backward Design serve as conceptual maps for planning or revising any course, syllabus, or lesson and can be easily adapted and mixed.

Effective teaching and learning frameworks emerge from psychological, cognitive, sociological, and educational research findings that students learn best when,

- the prior knowledge and "preconceptions" they bring into the classroom are recognized and engaged,
- they have practice and time to build "conceptual frameworks" upon foundational knowledge through active, experiential, and contextually varied learning and

- they have practice and time to "take control of their learning" through metacognitive reflection.

These frameworks often call for classroom activities integrating lectures with discussion, active learning, and self-reflection. L. Dee Fink writes that "A long history of research indicates lecturing has limited effectiveness in helping students,

- Retain information after a course is over
- Develop an ability to transfer knowledge to novel situations
- Develop skills in thinking or problem-solving
- Achieve effective outcomes, such as motivation for additional learning or a change in attitude."

Teaching and learning frameworks provide scaffolded, diverse approaches that help students "form knowledge structures that are accurately and meaningfully organized" while informing "when and how to apply the skills and knowledge they learn" (Ambrose et al.). Eschewing "Instruction," which focuses on content delivery, "Learning" focuses on structures for continual student development, inviting students to be "co-producers" in the classroom (Barr and Tagg). This page overviews significant teaching and learning frameworks, from theoretical and methodological approaches for overall course design to specific techniques for individual class sessions.

Examples of Course Design Frameworks

Course design frameworks provide models for achieving learning outcomes in overall courses, crafting the syllabus, and course redesign. Many elements in course design can also be applied to individual class design.

Backward Design

Backward Design originated with Wiggins and McTighe in their book, "Understanding by Design," and drives the educational philosophy behind most recent teaching and learning frameworks. Backward Design differs from classic beginning-to-end approaches to instructional design, where the instructor decides what content to teach before developing activities and assessments for the resulting learning. Backward Design instead begins with desired end goals by focusing on what the learner will learn rather than what the teacher will teach. In this sense, Backward Design is a student-centered approach.

The Backward Design process for designing instruction has three main stages:

- Identify desired results
- Determine acceptable evidence
- Plan learning experiences and instruction
- The corresponding actions are:
- Write student learning goals and learning outcomes
- Create assessments that measure progress toward outcomes
- Design activities that will prepare learners to perform well on the assessments

Instructors may choose the Backward Design process for several reasons:

- It is well supported by learning theory.
- It improves the attainment of desired learning outcomes.
- It is a well-known and widely accepted approach to course design.
- It is easy to remember and explain.
- It is transferable to almost any instructional situation.

Integrated Course Design

Integrated Course Design was developed by L. Dee Fink (2013) and expanded Backward Design into a detailed methodology specific to higher education. As its crucial feature, Integrated Course Design arranges the stages of Backward Design into a simultaneous planning strategy informed by environmental and contextual factors specific to higher education:

As part of its simultaneous methodology, Integrated Course Design guides instructors through a 12-step process for creating and aligning learning outcomes, classroom activities, rubrics, assessment protocols, and the syllabus in light of the context and potential challenges:

It also provides a detailed model for executing a Backward Course that considers environmental and contextual factors impacting student learning. Instructors may choose this framework to facilitate

Backward Design in their courses while including considerations of inclusivity and faculty-student assessment throughout the term.

Examples of Class Design Frameworks

Class Design Frameworks provide models for achieving learning outcomes in individual class sessions, developing activities, and motivating students. Some frameworks, like Universal Design for Learning, can also apply to course design.

5E Model

The Biological Sciences Curriculum Study developed the 5E model. The approach has been typically used in the sciences, but its principles can be applied to other disciplines (BSCS, 2001). 5E provides a 5-step strategy for designing individual lesson plans or class sessions: engagement, exploration, explanation, elaboration, and evaluation, which occurs throughout the cycle. Like many modern instructional frameworks, this approach is based on Constructivist Theory, wherein students learn by experiencing phenomena and reflecting upon their learning. During the first five minutes of class, the instructor uses an activity that engages students in learning and builds upon their prior knowledge.

This helps to scaffold new learning in ways that ascend Bloom's taxonomy, moving from comprehending to articulating and developing. The students might assess their understanding at the end of class, and the instructor may evaluate the learners on critical skills and concepts. Instructors may choose this model for its scaffolding approach, prioritization of student learning, and flexibility to occur once or multiple times within a class session.

Accelerated Learning Cycle

The Accelerated Learning Cycle was developed by Alistair Smith (1996). Like 5E, it can be used to structure single-class sessions. Accelerated Learning draws from Howard Gardner's theory of multiple intelligences by building a classroom that acknowledges varied prior knowledge and learning habits.

The model has several stages: the instructor creates a safe and welcoming learning environment, builds on the background knowledge of the learners to develop a larger contextual framework, describes intended learning outcomes, provides new information or content, facilitates a student activity, enables discussion or interactive demonstration based on the findings of the activity, and reviews and reinforces presented information.

Through these steps, ALC prioritizes "the needs of the learner" while "helping) students understand their learning preferences better" (Smith 1996).

Universal Design for Learning

Universal Design for Learning was developed in the early 1990s as a model for addressing the diverse learning needs of students in the classroom. It can be applied to course or single-class session designs, and its focus on accessibility makes it a practical approach to ensuring the success of class sessions for every student. UDL operates under three essential principles:

1. Provide Multiple Means of Engagement (the "why" of learning)
2. Provide Multiple Means of Representation (the "what" of learning)

3. Provide Multiple Means of Action and Expression (the "how" of learning)

These principles are also understood within UDL as approaches that, respectively, account for learning inquiries like "affective" (why?), "recognition" (what?), and "strategic" (how?). These spheres are flexible enough to modulate the level of challenge and positive experience in the classroom, providing a dynamic curriculum to address comprehensive student needs.

Instructors may incorporate UDL for its strategies on inclusivity and access and its wide-ranging recommendations for revising and varying teaching approaches. UDL provides "a sufficiently flexible curriculum so that each learner can find the right balance of challenge and support" (Meyer et al., 2014). The approach has classically been understood to improve environments for learners with disabilities, but its principles apply more broadly to creating inclusive classroom settings.

Recommendations

Identify the Most Relevant Framework: The applicability of teaching and learning frameworks will depend on various variables, including teaching philosophy, classroom environment, course objectives, student demographics, and challenges to teaching. Instructors can consider which elements from which frameworks are most relevant and helpful for use in their classrooms.

Create a Course Alignment Map: As illustrated in the figures above, instructors can create a map when designing a course. Doing so encourages instructors to align all items with the course's learning outcomes, avoiding more instructor-centered approaches to course development.

Assess Student Knowledge: Ascertaining prior knowledge and skills helps instructors craft a learning arc that fits and challenges specific student representations. Review syllabi from prerequisite courses to gauge likely student knowledge and recent reading; ask students to anonymously share their strengths and weaknesses on index cards on the first day of class or in an online survey before class; perform group brainstorming or focused keyword activities to uncover student knowledge.

Include Formative and Summative Assessments: Formative assessments help instructors monitor students' progression toward achieving learning outcomes and modify instruction as needed. Summative assessments are performed for the sake of accountability. As each of these types of evaluations serves specific purposes, both should be included within alignment maps.

Complete a Teaching Practices Inventory: An inventory can help instructors identify their teaching habits and explore the best frameworks for developing new habits, approaches, and course designs. Various inventories describe instructors' typical teaching approaches, many short and self-driven. The "Downloads" section at the bottom of this page also contains an assessment for considering degrees of inclusivity in syllabus and course design.

Modify Activities and Assessments as Needed: If students do not appear to be reaching the learning outcomes as desired, instructors can use feedback from the assessments and observations to reflect upon why this is the case. Activities and assessments may need to be modified to better prepare students for the outcomes.

10

AI WRITERS

Many content generation tools are available today, and I used a few of them to help write this book. Not all were tremendously useful, but I've included them because they hold potential for future projects. The following is a non-exhaustive description of some of the tools:

Sudowrite

The Describe feature can provide unique details for historical fiction writers. The Write function is a go-to tool when deadlines are approaching and can craft examples of what could come next. Guided Write is a close cousin to Write, providing story event ideas and allowing users to copy and paste the next story beat.

Once a good draft is created, the next step is to work with Rewrite, which comes with six presets and can be customized to add more dialogue or strengthen verbs. Sudowrite has been gaining popularity due to its updating AI algorithms and the development team's innovations. Two significant new tools have recently launched: First Draft and Shrink Ray.

First Draft costs the number of words in a document to shrink it down to loglines, a blurb, a summary, and an outline. Unlocking the essential Sudowrite functions, Write, Guided Write, Rewrite, and Describe, will immediately impact your current writing project.

Writing requires at least 20 words but works best with more. A crucial part of writing with Sudowrite is first feeding the computer some prompts. Software like Sudowrite takes the guesswork out of prompting, and most of the time, behind the scenes, the software asks the AI to help you write fiction. However, this does not mean you can't use Sudowrite to write nonfiction.

In your Write Settings, set your Creativity at three and ask for two cards of about 250 words. Sudowrite generates two cards on the right-hand side of your screen, highlighting the power of machine learning in the writing world. Machine learning is already changing the writing world, from neural networks writing poetry to AI generating music and photo captions.

If you're looking for a quick story and the AI doesn't interest you, check out Sudowrite's collection of short stories. However, there are problems with each card in Sudowrite, such as factual errors and the fact that the algorithms stopped learning in 2021. You would look foolish if you used the research generated by the AI card.

Both cards give an excellent example of a typical layout for an engaging blog post. To create a usable blog post using Write, revisit Key Details in Write Settings in the top left. Sudowrite is designed to help authors brainstorm ideas, flesh out characters, and suggest activities to advance the plot. The software can suggest topics to write about, help with research, and create outlines.

However, Sudowrite is not a replacement for the human imagination entirely. AI can assist with the creative process but cannot entirely replace the human imagination. For those considering using Sudowrite, it is essential to remember that the software is meant to supplement their writing, not a replacement for their creativity. With careful application, authors can use Sudowrite to their advantage and take their stories to the next level.

I didn't use Sudowrite for this book, but it's a good tool for creating story-based learning material.

Save the Cat

Save the Cat! The software helps writers structure and organize their stories effectively and grippingly by following "Save the Cat!" beats. This story structure method, created by screenwriter Blake Snyder, breaks down a story into 15 beats that emulate a hero's journey.

The software allows writers to:

- Set up character biographies to flesh out character arcs
- Identify and organize story beats to map the plot
- Create outlines and treatments for screenplays, novels, and short stories
- Track progress and flag unfinished portions of the story

Save the Cat software helps writers stay organized and on track by providing a framework and checklist. The visual story structure makes complex plotting easier to manage and helps ensure nothing falls through the cracks.

The software's beat sheets, character biographies, and outline templates provide a bird's eye view of the story, allowing writers to spot plot holes, weak character arcs, and areas for improvement earlier on. This leads to a more polished and cohesive final draft.

Save the Cat software is a valuable productivity tool for writers looking to optimize their process and produce high-quality stories with memorable characters and tightly-plotted narratives.

I explored this tool extensively because of its Beat Sheet based on Syd Field's Paradigm Structure but found it unusable for this book.

I hoped to create a linear flow to the book and avoid all References and Footnotes. These two screenplay-writing software gave me ideas for an undisturbed structure for the Tantra Learning Framework. Somehow, I managed to use the device of "flashbacks" to create the Chapters in a sequential flow.

The Appendices at the end of this book are "nice-to-have" information – they are not vital for the book's main idea.

Quillbot

Quillbot provides a variety of features that make it invaluable for content creators. It offers:

Grammatical error correction – Quillbot scans your text and fixes common mistakes like subject-verb agreement errors, pronoun usage issues, etc. This ensures that your content is polished and professional.

Improved readability – The AI rewords complicated phrases and sentences to make them easier for a broad audience to understand. This increases the readability and engagement of your content.

Synonym suggestions – Quillbot suggests alternative words that are more descriptive, varied, or conversational. This helps spice up repetitive phrases and make your writing more dynamic.

Plagiarism check – The tool scans your text against its database and the web to detect copied content, allowing you to refine and source your work correctly.

Overall, Quillbot helps writers produce high-quality, error-free, engaging copy with less effort. By leveraging its AI-based editing, you can create content that attracts, informs, and persuades your target audience.

I used this tool to summarize some research papers.

Grammarly

Grammarly helps writers improve their writing by quickly identifying spelling errors, grammatical mistakes, and plagiarism. It also offers context-sensitive suggestions to help communicate clearly and effectively.

Some of Grammarly's main features include:

- Checking spelling and grammar
- Identifying plagiarism
- Suggesting more readable and concise wording
- Providing context-sensitive word choices
- Highlighting overused or redundant phrases

Grammarly works with various writing tools like Google Docs, Microsoft Word, email clients, and social media platforms. You can use it for work documents, school assignments, email messages, etc.

Grammarly helps users:

- Express their ideas more clearly and concisely
- Avoid common grammatical mistakes
- Maintain a consistent tone and style throughout their writing
- Improve the overall quality and professionalism of their writing

Grammarly can be a valuable addition to any writer's toolkit. Catching errors that the human eye may miss can help improve the clarity, conciseness, and credibility of your writing.

I Love PDF

I love PDF, which offers a simple and intuitive platform for converting PDF files to editable Word documents. With just a few clicks, you can:

1. Upload your PDF

2. Choose your conversion settings like page range and layout

3. Download your converted Word file

The result is a .doc or .docx file that preserves the original formatting of the PDF as closely as possible. Tables, images, and other elements are converted so you can edit the text in Word.

The platform prides itself on providing highly accurate conversions with minimal data loss. Their advanced conversion algorithms are optimized to:

- Detect and preserve columns and tables
- Maintain fonts, font sizes, and styles
- Convert lists, hyperlinks, and bookmarks
- Transfer images and graphics

The result is a Word file that looks and feels very similar to the original PDF, allowing for a seamless editing experience.

It's an easy way to unlock the text in your PDFs. If you work with many PDF documents that you'd like to edit the text in, I Love PDF is a quick and effective solution. With a fast, high-quality conversion and a simple interface, it offers an easy way to extract the textual content from your PDFs and put it in a reusable Word file.

Canva

Canva is a fantastic book cover designing software. It can also help create unique infographics. It allows you to design social media posts, logos, greeting cards, and more. Its user-friendly interface lets you choose from thousands of templates and add images, fonts, and colors. This makes it a versatile and affordable design tool for beginners and professionals.

Some key features that make Canva stand out include:

- Hundreds of ready-made templates: Canva has templates for virtually any design need, from Facebook covers to Instagram posts to flyers and newsletters. This saves you time designing from scratch.

- Extensive image library: Canva has millions of free-to-use photos, illustrations, and icons. You can easily search for and insert the perfect visual elements into your designs.

- Easy customization: With simple drag-and-drop tools, you can move, resize, or adjust any design element. You can layer images, add filters, and apply effects to make your designs unique.

- Built-in fonts: Canva has hundreds of professional fonts built right in. Before inserting it into your design, preview how the text will look.

- Instant sharing: Once your design is complete, you can instantly download and share your creation on social media or via email with one click.

Canva's ease of use, wide range of templates, and robust feature set make it an ideal tool for instructional designers looking to create visual materials to complement their lessons and courses. Some ways Canva can help instructional designers include:

- Creating presentation slides with visually engaging images, diagrams, and animations to illustrate key concepts.
- Designing infographics to summarize complex topics and processes in an easy-to-understand visual format.
- Making worksheets, handouts, and activity templates for students during lessons. Canvas templates provide a good starting point that can be easily customized.
- Building e-learning assets like interactive quizzes, assessments, and multimedia content to bring lessons to life online. Canva has predesigned elements that can be dragged and dropped into designs.
- Producing posters, flyers, and other visuals to supplement instruction and reinforce key takeaways from lessons. Simple and impactful graphics can help cement new information in students' minds.

In summary, Canva's robust design tools and ease of use make it a valuable addition to any instructional designer's toolkit. The time saved by predesigned templates and the professional-looking results they enable can help instructional designers create engaging visual materials that enhance learning outcomes.

Quietquill

Quietquill's content generation is powered by advanced artificial intelligence models that can produce human-like text. Some of the main capabilities of Quietquill's content generation include the following:

Natural Language Flow

The software can continue content in a natural, flowing manner that sounds like human writing. There are no abrupt transitions or discontinuities in the generated text.

For instance, imagine a scenario where the software describes a recent vacation trip. It could generate text something like this:

"The weather was perfect as we walked along the beach, waves gently lapping at our feet. We spent hours exploring the tide pools, marveling at the urchins and anemones tucked into the rocks. As the sun set, we found the perfect spot to watch the sky turn orange and purple, listening to the seagulls calling overhead."

The text flows smoothly from one sentence to the next, with natural transitions and a consistent, human-written tone. There are no nonsensical jumps in the content or abrupt changes in the level of detail. The generated text paints a cohesive picture that helps the reader visualize the vacation experience.

Maintains Consistent Tone and Style

For instance, imagine a scenario where the software describes a recent family vacation. It could generate text something like this:

"The kids were thrilled as we pulled into the campsite, racing to claim the bunk beds they had been dreaming of for months. After setting up our tents and settling, we walked through the towering pine trees surrounding the campground. The fresh mountain air and sounds of wildlife put everyone in high spirits as we made plans for s'mores around the firepit and fishing at the nearby lake."

The generated text paints a cohesive picture of a fun family vacation experience through its consistent tone, level of detail, and sentence flow. The software imagines specific information that helps conjure the scene – the kids racing for the bunk beds, the towering pine trees, and plans for making s'mores and fishing – while maintaining an upbeat and enjoyable tone that continues naturally throughout the short passage.

Quietquill analyzes the input text to determine the appropriate tone, style, and word choice, then continues writing consistently with the same tone and vocabulary.

Handles Complex Topics

The AI models can generate content on various topics, from technology to business to history. It can research a topic and produce relevant, factually correct content.

For instance, imagine a scenario where the AI system is tasked with generating a summary of critical events in World War II. It could produce text like this:

"One of the most important events in World War II was Operation Barbarossa, in which Nazi Germany invaded the Soviet Union in June 1941. The invasion involved over 3 million Axis troops on the Eastern Front, making it the largest military operation in history. The invasion initially saw great success for the German forces, rapidly advancing into Soviet territory. However, Soviet resistance stiffened, and the German advance eventually stalled outside Moscow. The failure to defeat the Soviet Union in 1941 marked a turning point in the war, shifting the momentum in favor of the Allies."

The AI system can identify and describe the significant people, places, and events involved in World War II in an organized, factual manner. It provides relevant details about Operation Barbarossa – the scale of the invasion, the initial German gains, and the eventual stalling of their offensive – while maintaining an overall objective and factual tone appropriate for a summary of historical events.

Produces Readable Writing

The AI proofreads and rephrases the generated text to ensure it is readable, grammatically correct, and free of awkward phrasing or repetitions.

For example, imagine a scenario where the AI system generates a summary of critical events in designing an effective instructional program. It could produce text like this:

"One of the essential considerations in instructional design is defining clear learning objectives. Well-written objectives specify what learners will be able to do after completing instruction. Goals help guide the design of assessments, learning activities, and instructional strategies. Objectives should use action verbs that clearly describe the intended learning outcomes."

Another key event is analyzing learners and the context of the instruction. A needs assessment identifies what learners already know and can do and their required knowledge and skills. The analysis also considers learners' preferred styles, motivation, and environment. This information helps determine the appropriate instructional approach.

Selecting relevant instructional methods and media is also pivotal. Strategies may include direct instruction, inquiry-based learning, or collaborative group work. Various media like text, images, audio, video, and simulations can be integrated. The chosen methods and media should match learners' needs, preferences, and objectives.

Assessing learner achievement of the objectives represents a final critical event. Assessments provide feedback to learners and information to improve instruction. Formative assessments during instruction and summative assessments at the end are typically used. The assessments employ methods and media that match the objectives and learning activities."

The AI system can identify and describe essential considerations in designing an effective instructional program in an organized, factual manner. Quietquill offers a powerful yet easy-to-use solution for quickly generating large volumes of high-quality, human-like content.

Sometimes, I wish I could have written the Tantra Learning Framework using Quietquill. However, I could use only about 2% of what it generated.

Originality.ai

Originality.ai helps marketers produce high-quality, original content that resonates with their target audience. The tool uses artificial intelligence to check content for unintended plagiarism, repetition, and factual errors. This allows marketers to catch mistakes early and fix them before publishing content to their audience. Regularly using originality.ai can help improve a marketer's writing style by identifying overused phrases and recommending alternatives.

In addition to accuracy checks, originality.ai provides style insights that can make content more engaging and readable. The AI analyzes elements like sentence complexity, word choices, and tone to identify opportunities for improvement. Based on these insights, originality.ai often provides concrete suggestions marketers can implement to enhance their writing.

For instance, a corporate training team at a large financial institution could use originality.ai to improve the content of their training courses. First, they could run all existing course materials through the tool to detect unoriginal or incorrect content. This may reveal repeated phrases, factual errors, or unintended plagiarism from other training providers.

The team could then edit the problematic course content based on originality.ai's suggestions. They may also use style insights to make the language more engaging for trainees. They could integrate originality.ai into their process before publishing new course content. This would catch mistakes early and avoid the embarrassment of incorrect or plagiarized content being delivered to trainees.

Over time, as the team gets used to originality.ai's style recommendations, their training course content may become more unique and compelling in skill development. This could help improve key metrics like knowledge retention, trainee satisfaction, and productivity gains. By leveraging artificial intelligence to enhance their training content, the corporate team can create a better learning experience for their employees and maximize the impact of their training programs.

Originality.ai could also be used to improve the training materials for new employees at the financial institution. As part of the onboarding process, new hires receive various documents, checklists, and presentations introducing them to the company culture and their roles.

The onboarding team could run all of these materials through originality.ai to identify any areas for improvement. They may find that some documents use jargon-heavy or complex language that is hard for new employees to understand. Originality.ai could suggest simplifying the language and using more concrete examples.

The onboarding team could then edit the materials based on these style recommendations. They may break up long paragraphs, shorten sentences, and replace obscure terms with everyday words.

New onboarding materials created in the future could go through originality.ai as a matter of course. This would help ensure that all new hire training content is written in an engaging, accessible style that sets employees up for success from their first day on the job.

Pros

- New onboarding materials will be well-written in an accessible style.
- Employees will have a better first impression and understanding of the company.
- Knowledge retention and job performance may improve.

Cons

- There may be an initial time investment to run existing materials through the tool and make edits.
- Some employees may prefer materials written in a more technical style.
- The tool's recommendations must be reviewed carefully to avoid unintentionally changing the intended tone or meaning.

The onboarding team could also use originality.ai to improve the training materials for current employees. As employees progress in their roles, they often require additional training on new skills or processes.

The team could run existing training documents through originality.ai to identify ways to improve their effectiveness. For example, the tool may suggest:

- Adding more examples and visual elements to make complex concepts easier to understand
- Breaking training content into shorter sections to keep employees engaged
- Using more interactive exercises and assessments to improve knowledge retention

Any new training materials created in the future could then automatically pass through originality.ai's checks. This would help ensure consistent, high-quality, engaging training content for all employees as their roles evolve.

By leveraging artificial intelligence to analyze and improve its training materials, the company can create a culture of continuous learning where employees are set up for success in their current and future roles. Originality.ai can help identify opportunities to make training content more intuitive, accessible, and impactful, ultimately strengthening the company's human capital for long-term growth.

Hypotenuse

I used this tool extensively to write this book.

Hypotenuse lets you quickly generate fresh, unique, creative content that resonates with your target audience. Some of its best features include:

Simplicity: The interface is clean and intuitive, making it easy to use immediately.

For example, imagine you want to generate new blog content. All you have to do is open Hypotenuse, choose a topic and writing style, and enter a few starter words. Hypotenuse's AI engine will generate fresh, creative content based on your inputs. The interface guides you step-by-step through the process so there's no confusion.

Flexibility: You can generate content in various formats like paragraphs, bullet points, lists, etc.

For example, imagine you want to generate bullet point content for a social media post. With Hypotenuse's flexibility, you could:

1. Open the app and select 'Bullet Points' as the format
2. Enter a few starter words related to your industry

3. Click 'Generate'

Hypotenuse's AI engine will create 5-10 fresh, creative, and on-point bullet points for your post. The bullet points will:

- Be concise and scannable
- Focus on benefits for your audience
- Use an engaging tone

You can edit and copy the bullet points into your social media editor. The process would take only a few minutes, saving you time and effort versus writing the bullet points from scratch.

Creativity: The AI engine offers fresh and engaging suggestions to help you expand your content in new directions.

For example, imagine you're writing a blog post to showcase your company's latest product. You open Hypotenuse and select 'Product Description' as the writing style.

You enter a few starter words related to the product's key features and benefits. Hypotenuse's AI engine then generates new suggestions like:

- Its state-of-the-art widget utilizes advanced algorithms to optimize performance by up to 35%. Users will experience faster load times, smoother interactions, and more intuitive workflows.
- The ergonomic design promotes extended comfort while enabling higher precision and control. Users will appreciate the fatigue-reducing form factor and the intuitive button layout.

- An innovative cloud-based architecture allows for seamless updates that enhance security, compatibility, and functionality over the product's lifetime. Customers will have peace of mind knowing they always have the latest features.

You edit the suggestions to fit your voice and tone and expand on them to fully showcase your product's advantages. The fresh angles and compelling wording help give your blog post the engaging hook it needs.

Productivity: Hypotenuse saves you time by generating initial content drafts you can edit and customize to suit your needs.

Here is an experiment I tried with Hypotenuse. I told it to find similarities between Richard Dawkins and Vito Corleone. I felt this was in keeping with my concept that learning is all about making connections.

The similarities Hypotenuse highlighted provided an exciting perspective on the nature of power and influence.

> *Richard Dawkins and Vito Corleone achieved prominence through intelligence, strategic thinking, and an ability to inspire loyalty. However, they ultimately pursued their goals through very different means.*
>
> *Richard Dawkins spread his ideas through persuasion, evidence, and argument. He used his platform as an evolutionary biologist to promote atheism and rational thinking. Vito Corleone, on the other hand, ruled through fear, violence, and omerta.*

> *While Richard Dawkins changed minds through the power of ideas, Vito Corleone changed behavior through the power of coercion. Their differing approaches highlight that power can be wielded ethically or unethically, constructively or destructively.*

Still, Hypotenuse found a connection between the two figures through its broader conceptual framing. Sometimes, making unexpected comparisons can provide fresh perspectives and reveal commonalities that transcend surface differences. This experiment reinforced the value of finding linkages between seemingly disparate domains.

In another prompt, Hypotenuse found a personality such as Niccolo Machiavelli, who was immoral (like Vito Corleone) and an atheist (like Richard Dawkins). Indeed, Vito "Godfather" Corleone is a fictional character, but ideas are not compelled to be grounded in reality.

> *This highlights an important point about the ability of AI systems to find meaningful connections, even between fictional and real-world entities. While grounded in logic and evidence, their conceptual frameworks are not limited by strict adherence to factuality. This enables them to provide fresh perspectives that may not occur to humans constrained by real-world knowledge.*
>
> *Drawing connections between seemingly disparate domains is a crucial strength of AI systems. However, this can also pose risks if the systems generate incorrect or harmful associations. System developers must monitor for such issues and provide fact-checks or guidance to refine AI associations.*

Overall, my experiment with Hypotenuse demonstrated both the benefits and potential risks of AI's connectivity. On the positive side, their conceptual frameworks enabled interesting comparisons and relationships that expanded my thinking. But there is also a need for caution and oversight and a responsibility on developers to build AI systems that generate associations grounded in truth, ethics, and human values.

As the last line in the previous paragraph shows, Hypotenuse can get preachy.

Indeed, Hypotenuse's tendency towards grandiose statements and moralizing could sometimes get tiresome. However, we must remember that AI systems are still in their infancy, and Hypotenuse's "preachy" moments likely stem from its limited perspective and understanding of complex human issues. With proper guidance, feedback, and further training, AIs' propensity to preach could diminish as their knowledge and wisdom grow.

The onus remains for system developers and users to provide context, perspective, and balance when engaging with AI systems. We must view their outputs critically and refine their associations to minimize potential harm. At the same time, AI's ability to make unexpected connections can inspire new ideas and perspectives if harnessed responsibly. We can nurture AI systems with patience and prudence to become valuable tools that augment human capabilities while avoiding the most extreme risks of runaway preaching or harmful associations.

While Hypotenuse's preachiness highlights the limitations of current AI, with proper oversight and refinement, these systems can provide fresh insights that expand your thinking. The key will be developing AI to combine their connectivity and creativity with human wisdom and values.

Finally, Hypotenuse is worth checking out if you're looking for a content creation tool that's easy to learn, highly versatile, and helps spark your creativity. I would recommend trying the free version to experience the benefits for yourself!

11

FIVE POWERS OF GOD

This is not my invention; it is Tantra's. The Powers of God are named thus because they distinguish us from animals, even the higher-order ones.

1. Power of Consciousness

As I delve deeper into the essence of the Tantra Learning Framework, I cannot help but be captivated by the inherent power of wakeful awareness combined with self-awareness. This profound force can transform our lives and guide us on a spiritual journey of self-discovery and enlightenment.

The power of consciousness is intricately linked to the concept of wakeful awareness. It is the state of being fully present in the current moment, observing our thoughts, emotions, and sensations without judgment or attachment. This wakeful awareness allows us to connect with our true essence, tap into the depths of our being, and transcend the limitations of the material world. Within the realm of the Tantra Learning Framework, the power of consciousness is deeply intertwined with the transformational instructional design process.

Through wakeful awareness, we can break free from the shackles of our conditioned mindsets and expand our understanding of reality. It enables us to explore our belief systems, assumptions, and prejudices and question the underlying truths that govern our lives. We open ourselves to new perspectives, possibilities, and personal growth by embracing wakeful awareness.

This can revolutionize our approach to crafting meaningful learning experiences. Traditionally, instructional design has predominantly focused on transmitting knowledge and information. However, as we dive into the depths of the Tantra Learning Framework, we realize that authentic learning goes beyond acquiring facts and figures.

Wakeful awareness allows instructional designers to move beyond a purely cognitive understanding of learning, expanding their horizons to encompass the holistic development of the learner's mind, body, and collective unconsciousness. We can create transformative learning experiences that foster self-reflection, self-discovery, and self-mastery by infusing wakeful awareness into the instructional design process.

One of the fundamental principles of the Tantra Learning Framework is the recognition that authentic learning happens when we engage the whole being – mind, body, and spirit. Instructional design within this framework is not limited to information dissemination but encompasses a journey of self-realization and transformation. Wakeful awareness is pivotal in this process, allowing learners to tap into their inner wisdom, intuition, and innate potential.

We create an environment that fosters deep reflection and introspection by weaving wakeful awareness into instructional design. Learners are encouraged to explore their beliefs, values, and perspectives and critically examine the narratives that shape their lives. This reflective process facilitates personal growth, triggers self-awareness, and unlocks the untapped potential within each learner.

Incorporating the power of wakeful awareness into the instructional design also enhances the learner's ability to navigate complexity and uncertainty. In today's fast-paced world, where the only constant is change, learners must develop the skills to adapt, innovate, and think critically. Wakeful awareness cultivates the capacity to observe and respond to situations with clarity and discernment, empowering learners to make informed decisions and creatively navigate their challenges.

Furthermore, wakeful awareness elevates instructional design beyond mere knowledge consumption, transforming it into a transformative experience. Learners become active participants in their growth and transformation. They recognize that learning is not a passive endeavor but an opportunity for deep introspection.

In conclusion, the power of wakeful awareness is a profound force that can potentially transform our learning experience. We can transcend the limitations of our conditioned mindsets and tap into our inner wisdom.

2. Power of Bliss

The Power of Bliss, a core principle in Tantra, holds within it the key to unlocking the extraordinary potential within each of us. Ancient wisdom teaches us the meaning of happiness and provides us with a framework to pursue and cultivate it actively in our lives. With this profound knowledge, we can tap into the transformative power of bliss and redefine our understanding of what it means to be truly content and fulfilled.

Bliss is not limited to the fleeting moments of pleasure we often associate it with. Instead, it encompasses a more profound joy and fulfillment beyond the superficial. It is a state of being that transcends the ordinary and transports us to a realm where happiness becomes a way of life. The Power of Bliss, therefore, is not only about experiencing pleasure in a mundane sense but also about realization.

Tantra encourages us to explore and indulge in our desires to experience bliss and happiness. It teaches us that denying our desires is futile, for they are integral to who we are as human beings. Instead of suppressing or ignoring our desires, Tantra invites us to embrace them thoroughly and use them as a gateway to deeper levels of fulfillment and happiness.

However, it is essential to note that Tantra does not promote hedonism or mindless indulgence. Instead, it teaches us the art of discernment and conscious exploration. It invites us to examine our desires critically, understanding that not all desires are created equal. By cultivating self-awareness and understanding the true nature of our desires, we can separate the ones that lead us astray from those that carry the potential for true bliss.

The transformative power of bliss lies in its ability to release us from societal conditioning and self-imposed limitations. In pursuing happiness and fulfillment, we often find ourselves trapped in a web of external expectations and unrealistic standards. Tantra encourages us to break free from these constraints and embrace our authentic selves. It invites us to honor our unique desires and pursue the paths that resonate with our most profound sense of purpose and fulfillment.

Imagine a learning environment where students are not merely passive recipients of information but active participants in their growth and transformation. Tantra offers a framework to design instructional experiences beyond rote memorization and standardized testing. It opens up avenues for self-discovery and personal exploration, enabling students to tap into their unique sources of bliss and happiness. Think fun, edutainment, gamification, and learning for entertainment rather than learning!

In this transformation, learners are encouraged to reflect on their desires, values, and aspirations. They are given the tools to identify their true passions and align their learning journey with their authentic selves. By acknowledging and embracing their desires, students can chart their path and create a life that brings them joy and fulfillment.

The Power of Bliss in Tantra invites us to uncover the ability to experience true happiness and its transformative impact on our lives. It teaches us that happiness is not a mere fleeting emotion but a state of being that can be cultivated and nurtured. By embracing our desires, breaking free from societal conditioning, and aligning our learning journey with our authentic selves, we can create a transformative learning experience that unlocks our true potential.

3. Power of Free Will

The Power of Free Will is a fundamental aspect of Tantra that offers us the freedom to choose, act, and express ourselves. It is an indomitable force within us, waiting to be harnessed and utilized to its fullest potential. With its rich and ancient roots, Tantra has recognized the immense power of Free Will and has integrated it into its teachings and practices.

In the realm of Tantra, Free Will is not merely a concept or an idea to ponder but rather a living and breathing force that permeates all other powers and gives them potency. The fuel ignites the fire of transformation, propelling us forward on our tantric journey and shaping our reality in profound ways.

The importance of Free Will in Tantra cannot be overstated. It is unequivocal about its existence and its significant role in our lives. Tantra recognizes that we are not bound by fate or predetermined paths but rather have the ability to exercise our Free Will to make choices and decisions that shape our destiny.

The Power of Free Will allows us to choose for or against something, to act or not to act, and to express ourselves or remain still/quiet. It is the cornerstone of our autonomy and personal agency, empowering us to take charge of our lives and shape our reality according to our desires and aspirations.

The Power of Free Will assumes even greater significance in the Tantra Learning Framework context. It becomes a pivotal element in the transformation of instructional design, as it provides a platform for learners to exercise their agency and actively participate in their learning journey.

By recognizing and honoring the Power of Free Will, the Tantra Learning Framework creates a space where learners are not passive recipients of knowledge but active participants in their learning process. It acknowledges that learners have unique perspectives, experiences, and individual needs that must be considered when designing instructional experiences.

In the realm of instructional design rooted in Tantra, the Power of Free Will is not suppressed or disregarded but embraced and harnessed. The framework recognizes that learning is a deeply personal and transformative process, so learners should be given the freedom and autonomy to shape their learning experiences.

The Power of Free Will in the Tantra Learning Framework goes beyond the traditional instructional design model, often focusing on prescribing a one-size-fits-all approach. Instead, it encourages instructional designers to create a flexible and adaptable learning environment that respects and supports the learner's individuality and strengths.

This paradigm encourages learners to explore their interests, follow their passions, and chart their learning path. They are given the agency to choose the topics they want to delve deeper into, the resources they want to explore, and the pace at which they wish to progress. This freedom to choose, act, and express themselves fosters a sense of ownership and empowerment, enabling learners to take charge of their learning journey.

Furthermore, the Power of Free Will in the Tantra Learning Framework also recognizes the transformative potential of self-reflection and introspection. It encourages learners to pause, reflect, and evaluate their experiences, thoughts, and actions and to make conscious choices that align with their values and aspirations.

In the context of the Tantra Learning Framework, it assumes a central role in the transformation of instructional design, enabling learners to exercise their agency and actively participate in their learning journey. The Tantra Learning Framework empowers learners to explore their passions, make conscious choices, and ultimately shape their reality by harnessing the Power of Free Will and creating a learning environment that honors and supports individual autonomy.

4. Power of Knowing

At its core, knowledge is the ability to distinguish between belief, fact, and fiction. It is the foundation upon which our understanding of the world is built. Without knowledge, we would be adrift in a sea of uncertainty, unable to navigate the complexities of life. Tantra, I discovered, places great emphasis on the power of knowing and understanding. It recognizes knowledge as a potent tool for personal and collective transformation.

But what exactly constitutes knowledge? Is it simply a collection of facts and information? Or is there something more to it? As I delved deeper into this question, I realized that knowledge is not a fixed entity but a dynamic interplay of beliefs, truths, and experiences. It is the overlap of these elements that gives rise to proper understanding.

With its holistic approach to learning, Tantra offers the opportunity to expand one's knowledge and discern the truth. It encourages us to question our preconceived notions and challenge the boundaries of our beliefs.

However, it is essential to recognize that knowledge has its limitations. It is not the ultimate truth but a tool to help us make informed decisions. We must be open to the idea that our knowledge may be incomplete or flawed. Tantra teaches us to embrace this uncertainty and strive for a deeper understanding of ourselves and our world.

One research study revealed that individuals with a well-rounded knowledge base were more creative and innovative. They were also more likely to recognize cynicism within themselves before others pointed it out. This sheds light on the transformative potential of knowledge. By broadening our understanding of different subjects and disciplines, we open ourselves up to new perspectives and possibilities.

This means creating learning environments that foster collaboration and knowledge exchange in the instructional design context. By encouraging students to engage in dialogue, debate, and reflection, we can create a rich tapestry of knowledge that goes beyond individual perspectives and biases.

But how do we ensure that our knowledge is accurate and trustworthy? Tantra offers a framework for discerning truth through the cultivation of wisdom. It teaches us to question and scrutinize information and to separate fact from fiction. By cultivating this discernment, we can navigate the vast ocean of knowledge with clarity and confidence.

5. Power of Action

As I delve deeper into the Tattvas and their transformative potential, I cannot overlook the immense power of action. Through my journey of exploration and discovery, I have realized that action is not merely a means to an end but a catalyst for change and transformation. We manifest our desires and intentions through action, turning them into tangible reality. We uncover our true potential and bring forth our innate abilities within the depths of action. By understanding and harnessing this power, we can bring about profound shifts in our lives and the lives of others.

Imagine a scenario where learners are given the tools and guidance to absorb and implement information. This experiential approach solidifies their understanding and empowers them to apply their knowledge in real-life situations. The transformation from passive recipients of information to active agents of change is a remarkable journey that the Power of Action can facilitate.

Through the Tantra Learning Framework, we can adopt a unique and holistic approach to instructional design that goes beyond the limitations of traditional methods. By emphasizing the Power of Action, we create a learning environment that encourages exploration, experimentation, and discovery.

One way to incorporate the Power of Action into instructional design is through gamification. Gamified experiences have gained significant traction in recent years as they make learning engaging, interactive, and dynamic. We tap into the innate human desire for challenge and achievement by designing instructional materials in games or simulations. Learners become active participants, driven by their desire to succeed and progress within the game. In this scenario, action becomes the driving force behind both learning and transformation.

Imagine a language learning program that transforms into an immersive adventure, where learners actively engage with the language through quests, challenges, and interactive scenarios. Instead of simply memorizing vocabulary and grammar rules, learners are encouraged to use their newly acquired knowledge to complete tasks, communicate with virtual characters, and navigate different cultural contexts. The Power of Action, in this case, transforms language acquisition from a mundane chore into an exciting and transformative journey.

Another way to incorporate the Power of Action is through project-based learning. We create a bridge between theory and practice by assigning learners real-world projects that require them to apply their knowledge. Learners become active creators, using their newfound understanding to solve complex problems, design innovative solutions, and navigate unpredictable situations. The transformative power of action is at its peak in project-based learning, as it allows learners to witness firsthand the impact of their actions.

Consider a business management course where students create a business plan for a hypothetical startup. They must research market trends, study competitors, analyze financial data, and craft a comprehensive strategy. Through this project, they gain a deep understanding of business principles and develop essential skills such as critical thinking, problem-solving, and teamwork. The Power of Action, in this case, transforms passive learners into proactive entrepreneurs ready to embark on their ventures.

In conclusion, the transformative power of action is vital to the Tantra Learning Framework. By embracing the Power of Action in instructional design, we create engaging and impactful learning experiences that empower learners to take charge of their transformation. Whether through gamified experiences or project-based learning, the action becomes the vehicle through which learners manifest their desires and intentions. It is through action that we truly become the architects of our destiny and unlock the full potential of our being.

12

TANTRA LEARNING FRAMEWORK

Levels 11 to 7: Cause and Effect, Time, Desire, Knowledge, Action

The Intellectual Tattvas

In spirituality, reasoning and formal education are considered anathema to enlightenment or bliss or what have you. In this context, they are the Veils of Ignorance, with Maya or Illusion (sitting atop Level 6) being the Cloak of Ignorance.

There is, however, another way to look at this.

> *All reasoning and rational thought parameters are limited simply because we can't have all the information required to draw absolute conclusions. All learning is temporary, and cause-and-effect observations merely take specific observations to make broad generalizations.*

This serves us well within the limited span of human cognition – whether it's solving a minor problem or a multi-year project.

11. Cause and Effect

Intelligence helps us distinguish between objects and processes. It concludes its observations. It sees action and the effect of that action and makes universal statements about the same. It seems every action has a reaction and decides that that action will always cause that reaction! Hence, we all know about "cause and effect," and our lives run on it.

For example, if you leave a glass of water in the sun, the water will heat up and evaporate due to the sunlight. This is an example of cause and effect – the sunlight (cause) leads to the evaporation of the water (effect). We see cause-and-effect relationships all around us, from the fundamental physical interactions in the world to more complex social and psychological phenomena.

To give you an idea, if you forget to set your alarm clock, you will likely oversleep and be late for work. Forgetting to set the alarm (cause) leads to oversleeping and being late (effect). Your boss getting upset with you for being late would also be an effect of not setting the alarm correctly.

As proof, observe your daily activities and interactions. Multiple effects follow for every action you take – from making coffee to conversing with a friend. Cause and effect permeates our entire experience at this level of existence – the human psychological level of existence.

However, we never stop thinking about a particular action's cause.

If I light a match and take it to firewood (action), the wood will catch fire (reaction). Going deeper, why can't I consider the lighting of the match as a reaction? What was the cause? Why did I light the matchstick? OK! I was feeling cold. Why was I feeling cold? Is it because it is cold outside? Why is it cold outside? Because it is winter? And so on…

The entire business of cause-and-effect crumbles because of this endless regression into causality. Chaos Theory demonstrates how actions can cause disproportionate reactions and even no reaction whatsoever. It also tells us how reactions can occur with no evident action.

Will my training program have its desired effect?

10. Time

To be precise, this level deals with our perception of the forward movement of time. We say it rained for an hour if it rained from 3 pm to 4 pm. We cannot travel back in time, except, of course, in Science Fiction!

Imagine you want to travel back in time to meet your younger self. No matter how hard you try, it is impossible using current technology. Time only seems to move in one direction – forward. Causality would have significant paradoxes and implications even if we could travel back in time.

For instance, suppose you returned to your younger self and gave some advice. When you return to the present, your life may have changed drastically based on that advice. But if your life changed, would you have had a reason to travel back in time in the first place?

The very act of changing the past could prevent the future event that caused you to travel back. This creates a paradox. We can discuss *Back to the Future* endlessly and even find solace in the fact that multiple universes void all paradoxes of time travel. Still, as an experience or sensation, time is subjective.

In learning, I don't know when learning has occurred. I also don't know when it will occur if it occurs at all. I don't know how much time should be devoted to a particular learning task and my seat time for a module of instructional material.

Should I devote much time crafting an MMCQ assessment for a learning objective drafted at the Synthesis Level of Blooms?

Our perception of time as moving in one direction – from past to present to future – seems fundamental to how we experience reality. Traveling back in time highlights some strange implications of trying to alter the past from our present perspective.

In tantric visualization, I can "feel" the sensations of a past event! No empirical parameters fix an event in time; nothing stops me from returning to that experience. Time moves forward, but my subjective experience can travel in any direction! When tantriks say they can travel in time, they mean (because of visualization and vivid imagination techniques) that the experience is as accurate as when they had in the past.

How do we employ these techniques in the context of creating learning material?

9: Desire

We have learnt from Maslow that humans aspire to be bigger, better, smarter, faster. Desire encompasses all the psychological parameters below it. It is the superset of all the tattvas we have spoken of.

How do we embed this tattva within the learning design and development methodologies?

Imagine a large corporation that offers its employees all sorts of training programs. Courses on management, communication skills, software training, and so on help employees develop skills that benefit themselves and the company. Employees have every opportunity to gain knowledge and expertise that can advance their careers while the company benefits from a more skilled and productive workforce.

The training programs attempt to foster a culture of learning and growth within the organization. The company values employees who feel their development are more motivated and loyal.

But is it a given that employees will be motivated to partake in the training programs enthusiastically?

8. Knowledge

Knowledge has become a commodity that many seek to acquire and accumulate. It can be bought and sold in the marketplace of ideas, accessed through various media, and shared over the Internet at unprecedented speed and scale.

On the positive side, the global flow of information has increased knowledge accessibility for many. New technologies have made it easier than ever before to gain and spread knowledge. This diffusion of knowledge has the potential to alleviate poverty, solve complex problems, and drive innovation.

A student who studies diligently to gain knowledge from her textbooks and teachers manifests that motivation by getting good grades and securing a high-paying job after graduation. While there is nothing inherently wrong with these goals, they reflect a view of knowledge as a commodity to be acquired for material gain.

This view may not serve the student because she ought to study for the intellectual pleasures of literacy. But it serves the corporate employee because it helps to articulate that knowledge in terms of better pay, higher bonuses, and ease of doing work. The corporate creature benefits greatly by reducing knowledge to a commodity, pursuing it solely for material gain.

7. Action

My interpretation of this tattva is "execution."

The actions we take, however small, have ramifications. Even a simple gesture like smiling at a stranger can brighten their day and set positive events in motion. Conversely, acting in haste or with ill intent can cause harm and perpetuate suffering. This is not a trivial bit of information. I was told to smile more during an appraisal discussion at one of my earlier companies.

We think, we create, but we don't execute to our fullest potential. This is the message that Larry Bossidy and Ram Charan give us through their book, "Execution: The Discipline of Getting Things Done."

In my view, most training programs I created were around acquiring knowledge – very little thought was put into effectively implementing the new skills at the workplace. No wonder the direct correlation between a company's training programs and profits is only around 35 percent.

Can we use the Tantra Learning Framework to measure the success of a training program before the program is rolled out?

Tattvas versus Qualia

Tattvas are universal experiences of reality, while Qualia are subjective experiences of reality. Tattvas describes the essential properties and constituents of the universe, the fundamental principles that structure our experiences. They include concepts like space, time, consciousness, and self (among the 36 tattvas).

Qualia, conversely, refers to the qualitative "what it's like" aspects of our subjective experience – the redness of red, the sourness of sour.

Tattvas represent a more "objective" layer of reality, while Qualia are inherently "subjective." They are complementary but distinct – Tattvas describes the underlying framework, and Qualia fills it with subjective feeling and meaning. Together, they give us a more complete picture of the nature of consciousness and perception.

Pros

- Provides a more comprehensive view of reality by considering both objective and subjective aspects
- Gives insight into the relationship between the universal structures of experience and individual perception

Cons

- The distinction may be somewhat blurry and hard to define in practice
- The subjective nature of Qualia makes them difficult to study scientifically in an objective way

To illustrate with a metaphor, Tattvas can be likened to a machine's hardware – they provide the basic structure and components. Qualia are like the software – they give the hardware meaning and purpose through the experiences they generate. Neither is "more fundamental" – they are two sides of the same coin, inseparable in shaping our nature as perceiving beings.

To illustrate with a concrete example, imagine the sight and the experience of color. The fundamental properties of sight – like spatial perception, light, and form – correspond to the tattvas of space, time, and consciousness. They provide the basic framework for visual experience. But the actual colors we see – the red of an apple or the blue of the sky – are qualia. They fill that framework with subjective feeling and meaning. We couldn't experience "red" without the underlying tattva of space to locate it, but the specific, private sensation of redness is quale. Together, tattvas and qualia give rise to the richness and intricacy of our visual consciousness.

To illustrate with a different example, consider the experience of hearing a musical note. The fundamental properties of hearing – like the ability to perceive pitch, loudness, and timbre – correspond to the tattvas of space, time, and consciousness. They provide the basic framework for auditory experience. But the quale of "middle C" – the way that notes sound privately in our mind – is a quale. It fills that framework with a particular subjective sensation. We couldn't perceive the note middle C without the auditory tattvas that identify and locate it, but the way middle C sounds to us as individuals is a quale. Together, the tattvas and qualia of hearing give rise to our rich auditory experiences of music and the world.

The distinction between tattvas and qualia is an important one that helps illuminate the nature of consciousness. While tattvas provide the structural framework for experience, qualia give experience unique richness and subjectivity. Together, they work in tandem to shape how we perceive and interact with the world.

To continue the metaphor, we could say that qualia are like the colors, textures, and sensations that bring a machine's software to life. They give the tattvas meaning by imbuing them with feeling and lived experience. Without qualia, the tattvas would remain abstract structures devoid of the subjective character that makes conscious perception vivid and ineffable.

The study of qualia also points to the limitations of a purely materialistic or reductionistic approach to consciousness. While science can describe the tattvas that underlie experience, it struggles to fully account for the first-person, private sensations we refer to as qualia. This shows that a complete understanding of the mind will likely require perspectives beyond the purely physical or third-person.

In summary, the distinction between tattvas and qualia helps highlight critical aspects of consciousness. The tattvas provide the structural components, while the qualia fill those structures with subjective feeling. Together, they interact in complex ways to shape our rich inner lives and perceptions of the world. The study of qualia also points to limitations in purely physical explanations of the mind, showing that a comprehensive approach to consciousness will likely incorporate first-person perspectives. This distinction can thus further our understanding of the mind while reminding us of what remains mysterious.

As we explore consciousness scientifically, mapping the Tattvic and Qualic layers of experience will be crucial. Each reveals essential truths, and together, they may help us understand the deepest mysteries of the mind.

13

VISUAL REPRESENTATIONS

The 36 Tattva System of Non-Dual Kashmir Tantra

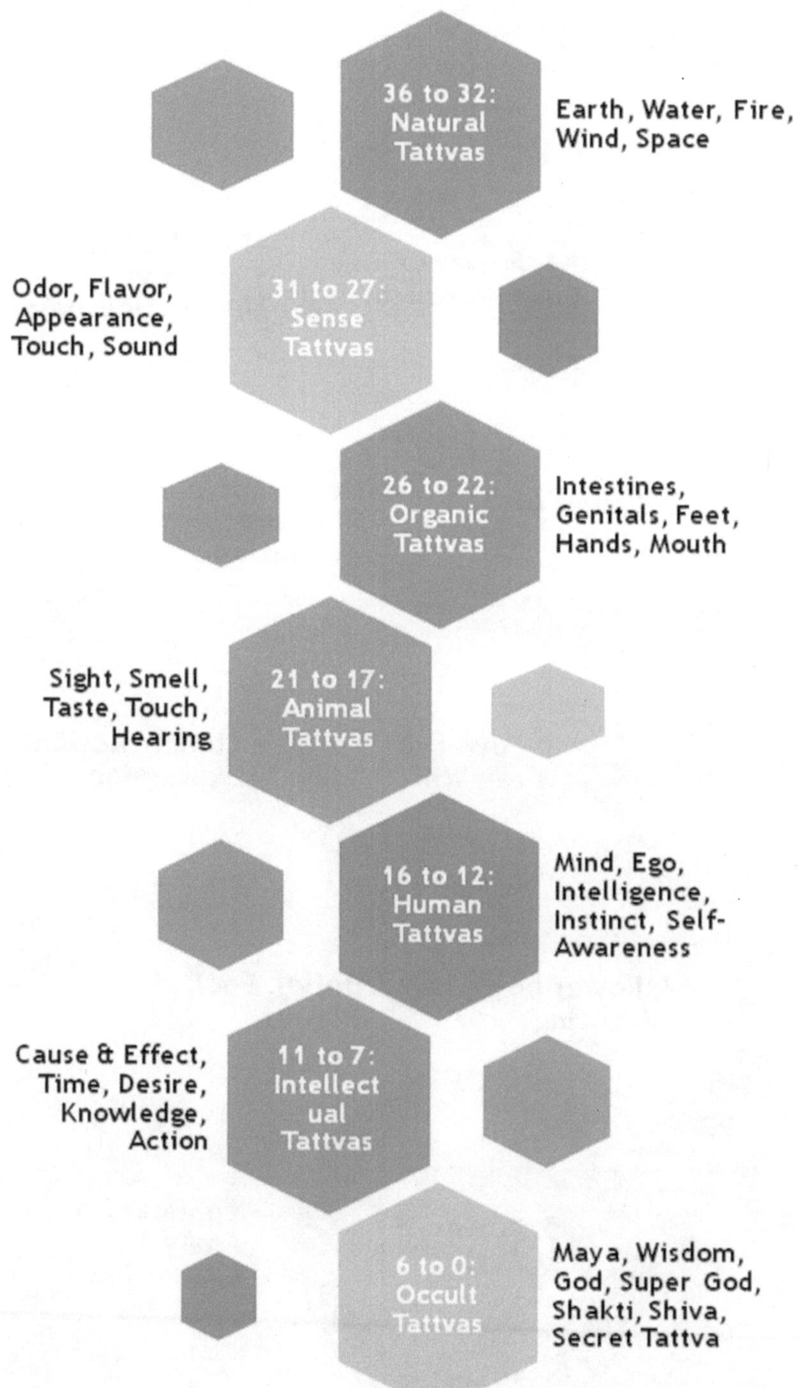
36 to 32: Natural Tattvas
Earth, Water, Fire, Wind, Space
31 to 27: Sense Tattvas
Odor, Flavor, Appearance, Touch, Sound
26 to 22: Organic Tattvas
Intestines, Genitals, Feet, Hands, Mouth
21 to 17: Animal Tattvas
Sight, Smell, Taste, Touch, Hearing
16 to 12: Human Tattvas
Mind, Ego, Intelligence, Instinct, Self-Awareness
11 to 7: Intellect ual Tattvas
Cause & Effect, Time, Desire, Knowledge, Action
6 to 0: Occult Tattvas
Maya, Wisdom, God, Super God, Shakti, Shiva, Secret Tattva

Powers of God

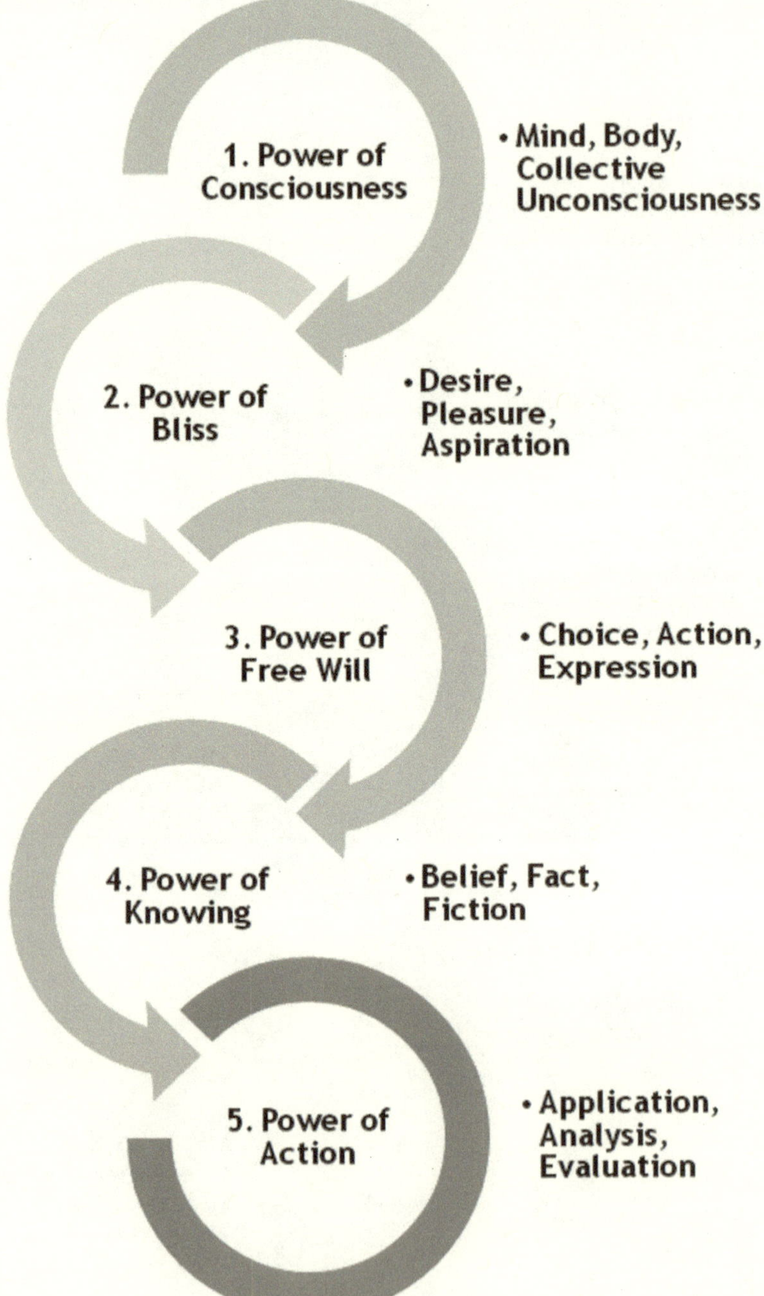

Visualization of an LO Using the Tantra Learning Framework

TANTRA LEARNING FRAMEWORK

Visualizing a Learning Object

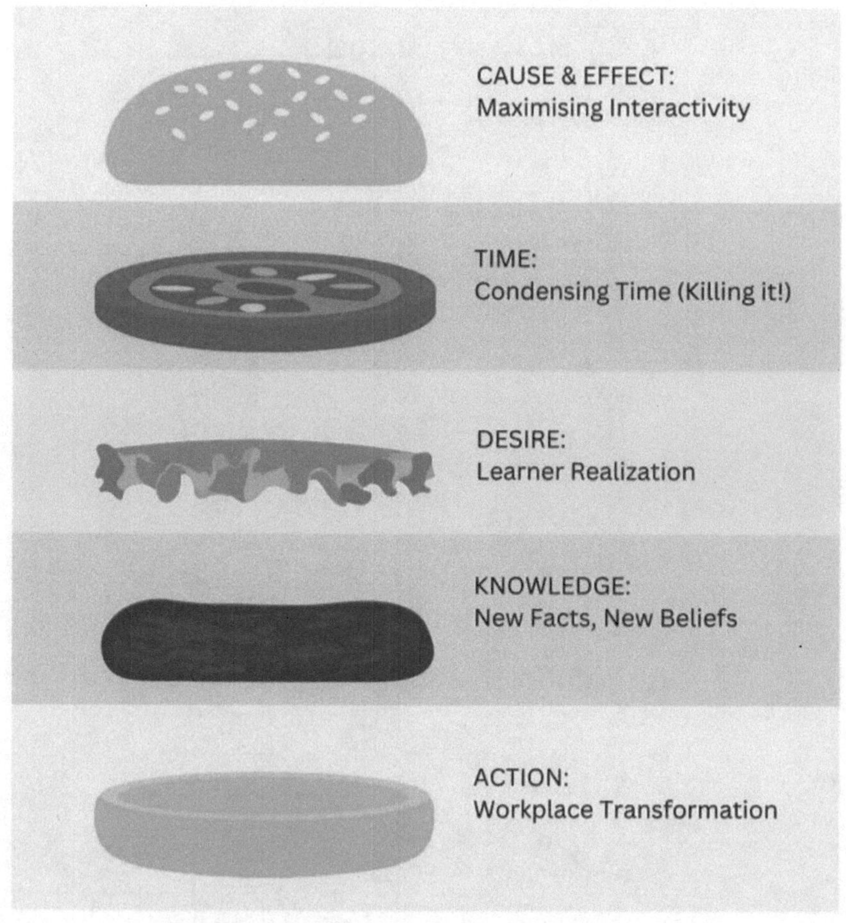

Tantra Learning Framework

TANTRA LEARNING FRAMEWORK

1. MAYA - ILLUSION

What is the ignorance?
What is the performance gap?
What training intervention is required?

2. CAUSE & EFFECT

What has caused the performance gap?
What is the anticipated effect?
Are the cause and effect aligned?

3. TIME

What is the required effort?
What is the time and money analysis?

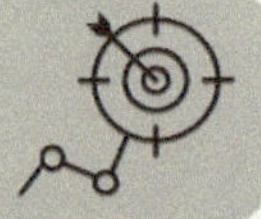

4. DESIRE

What is the desired action post learning?
Is the desire aligned with the learner's ego?

5. KNOWLEDGE

What is the nature of the knowledge object?
What is the knowledge check strategy?

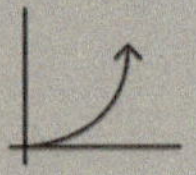

6. ACTION

What are the manifestions of action?

7. MAYA - ILLUMINATION

Have the Veils of Ignorance been lifted?

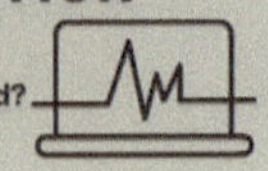

FUTURE ACTION

The proof of any pudding is in its eating! Tantra Learning Framework as an instructional design methodology can merit value only if its manifestations are helpful and practical. In this context, I hope to implement this across different clients, diverse projects, and over at least 1000 hours of learning.

I aim to measure its impact both qualitatively and quantitatively. On the qualitative side, I will seek feedback from learners, instructors, and managers on parameters like engagement, pleasure of learning, and reduced development time. On the quantitative side, I will track metrics like completion rates, knowledge retention, and time taken for performance manifestation.

Of course, there will be challenges, too. Instructional design is as much an abstract science as it is a science involving intuition, creativity, and human connection. The methodology must remain flexible to adapt to the context while retaining its fundamentals.

The biggest challenge will be the cost associated with its adoption, and I want to overcome this barrier by offering $1000 for 10 fully developed Learning Hours.

Additionally, I am optimistic about the potential of this approach. The Tantra Learning Framework can bring fresh air to corporate learning if implemented thoughtfully and iteratively. As I said at the start, the actual test lies in how helpful it proves in reality.

I look forward to that journey and hope to report back on learnings and improvements along the way. Perhaps "10 Hours – 100 Clients – 1000 Dollars" can be the title of my next book on the Tantra Learning Framework.

Appendices

Appendix I: Five States of Awareness

In Tantra Yoga, there are four states of awareness depending on how awake or sleepy we are. The fifth state is a state of awareness that needs cultivation: one must practice hard to discover or create it. Of the five states of understanding, we see four through waves of an EEG (electroencephalogram), corresponding to states of wakefulness/sleepiness.

1. Wakeful State

This is the state of awareness when we are awake. Beta waves correspond with this state; these are low-amplitude waves with a high frequency (over 14 cycles per second). We are most excitable in our wakeful state because we are active physically and mentally.

However, Tantra Masters have called this the least awakened state because we go about our daily chores and everyday life like automatons. Perhaps even like animals who engage only with simple entertainment, food, sleep, and excretion.

Simply because we are awake and active does not mean we are in the most "aware" state.

2. Relaxed State

When we are not engaged in intense physical or mental activity, we are in a Relaxed State. Alpha waves of the EEG correspond to this state of awareness, and they have frequencies ranging from 8 to 13 cycles per second. Some types of meditation that help you relax and de-stress enable you to reach this state of awareness. I mention only "some types of meditation" because other types can excite you.

3. The Dream State

All these states of awareness are continuous, so you will notice a hypnotic state before entering the dream state. You can experience this if you remind yourself to "look for it" before falling asleep. Your thoughts become nonsensical, and you may hear voices/sounds or feel entirely imaginary sensations but feel real. These sounds/sensations are hypnagogic hallucinations.

Don't worry; these are pretty normal. This is a transitory state between the Relaxed State and the Dream State. Theta waves correspond to this state and have a frequency of 4 to 7 cycles per second. From the frequency, it should be clear that lower frequencies show lower mental activity. This does not mean diminished mental capacity! It implies greater focus and greater concentration.

Some drugs slow mental processes or make us feel like everything is happening slowly. They also heighten our sensory perceptions. With practice, Tantra can help you achieve this state without drugs. Many tantriks today want to accomplish these mental states through shortcuts, so they resort to drugs. Their success is short-lived, and the physical damage caused by drug usage is apparent.

4. Deep Sleep State

Delta waves correspond to this state of awareness; they have high amplitudes and frequencies below four cycles per second. This is a state of unawareness in the physical sense and is the diametric opposite of the Wakeful State. This is complete "relaxation" in the genuine sense of the word. There are no dreams; you will achieve this state if you diligently practice Shavasana. Thus, if you want to achieve Delta waves, get a good night's rest.

5. Permeating All Four States

Beyond the Fourth State of Awareness, and simultaneously within each state of awareness, lives the Fifth State. This state does not lie on a scale, but one can say, "… is the scale itself." It makes little sense if you do not experience it, and because it is in the domain of the Occult, it remains indescribable. However, you can comprehend it in the following manner: The mind is twisted, strained, tortured or relaxed, stilled, quieted, calmed… to invent an uncommon state of awareness.

That is how Tantra works! Remember, Tantra comes from two words: tanoti (expand) and trayate (liberate). Expanded consciousness is as infinite as space, so there is no limit to altering or raising one's consciousness.

Appendix II: Five Acts of God

1. Self-Expression

In the world of Tantra, self-expression is a crucial aspect that holds immense transformative power. We tap into our innate creativity through self-expression, allowing our authentic selves to shine. It catalyzes personal growth and empowerment, enabling us to shape our reality and connect uniquely and profoundly with the world.

In the Tantra Learning Framework, self-expression is embraced and applied to instructional design. Traditionally, instructional design focuses on delivering information and knowledge in a structured manner, often neglecting the individuality and uniqueness of the learner. However, by incorporating self-expression into instructional design, we can create a learning experience that is engaging, personalized, and transformative.

Imagine a classroom where students are encouraged to express themselves freely and their thoughts, ideas, and emotions are valued and respected. This is a classroom where the power of self-expression is unleashed, allowing learners to take ownership of their learning journey and actively participate in their growth and development.

When self-expression is infused into instructional design, learners are not just passive recipients of knowledge but active co-creators of their learning experience. They are provided a platform to explore their passions, voice their opinions, and dive deep into their inner world of creativity. This fosters a sense of autonomy and agency and encourages learners to think critically, problem-solve, and engage in meaningful discussions.

As instructional designers, our role is not just to impart knowledge but to facilitate the process of self-discovery and self-expression. By honoring the uniqueness of each learner and creating space for them to express themselves authentically, we empower them to discover their truths and shape their reality in alignment with their values and aspirations.

The power of self-expression is not limited to the individual learner but extends to the collective learning environment. When learners are encouraged to express themselves freely, it fosters a sense of community and belonging. It creates a safe and inclusive space where diverse perspectives are celebrated, fostering a culture of openness, understanding, and empathy.

Incorporating self-expression into instructional design can take various forms. For instance, they allow learners to choose topics that resonate with them for assignments or projects, encourage them to present their work in creative formats such as art, music, or storytelling, or provide opportunities for collaborative and interactive activities that promote self-reflection and discussion. By diversifying instructional methods and creating a holistic learning experience, learners can express themselves in ways that align with their unique talents and abilities.

The transformational power of self-expression is not to be underestimated. Learners who are given the space and support to express themselves authentically deepen their understanding of the subject matter and cultivate a deeper connection with their inner selves. This connection allows them to tap into their inherent creativity, unleashing many ideas and possibilities.

As instructional designers, we harness this power and facilitate a learning environment that nurtures self-expression. This requires a shift in mindset from a rigid, one-size-fits-all approach to one that is flexible, adaptable, and responsive to the needs and desires of individual learners. It requires us to step out of the traditional boundaries of instructional design and explore new avenues that foster self-expression and creativity.

In conclusion, self-expression is a fundamental aspect of Tantra that can be applied to instructional design in the Tantra Learning Framework. By incorporating self-expression into instructional design, we empower learners to tap into their creative potential, shape their reality, and engage in a meaningful and transformative learning experience.

The power of self-expression can revolutionize traditional instructional design methods and create a more engaging, personalized, and empowering learning environment. Let us embrace the power of self-expression and embark on a journey of self-discovery, creativity, and transformation.

2. Preservation

Preservation is an essential aspect of the Tantra Learning Framework, as it enables individuals to create a solid foundation to build upon. In pursuing personal growth and self-improvement, it is crucial to maintain a state of mind that aligns with one's highest potential. This requires a concerted effort to preserve and nurture this state, ensuring its longevity and stability.

Throughout history, various spiritual traditions and philosophies have recognized the importance of preservation in self-realization.

The ancient teachings of Tantra, for instance, emphasize the need to cultivate an unwavering focus on one's objectives. This encompasses the physical and mental aspects of being, as the mind plays a crucial role in shaping our experiences and determining our reality.

Preservation entails safeguarding the clarity of the mind and protecting it from distractions, negative influences, and destructive thoughts. It is about cultivating a positive mental environment where our thoughts and emotions are harnessed toward our highest potential. Through consistent effort and practice, we can develop the ability to maintain a state of mind that empowers us and propels us toward personal transformation.

To effectively preserve our state of mind, it is essential to develop a self-awareness that allows us to recognize and address any challenges or obstacles that may arise. This requires a deep understanding of our thoughts, emotions, and behavior patterns. By becoming aware of these aspects of ourselves, we can consciously cultivate thoughts and emotions that align with our goals and aspirations.

A key aspect of preservation is the ability to meditate and cultivate mindfulness. Meditation lets us quiet the mind, detach from external distractions, and connect with our inner consciousness. This practice will enable us to observe our thoughts and emotions without judgment and better understand ourselves and our reactions to the external world.

In the Tantra Learning Framework context, preservation also involves nurturing the body and the physical environment. Our physical well-being plays a significant role in our mental and emotional states. Therefore, engaging in activities promoting health, such as exercising regularly, eating a balanced diet, and getting enough rest, is crucial.

Caring for our bodies creates a strong foundation for preserving our mental and emotional well-being.

Furthermore, the physical environment we live and work in can significantly impact our state of mind. Cluttered and chaotic spaces can create unnecessary mental and emotional stress, hindering our ability to maintain a state of calm and clarity. We create an environment conducive to preservation and growth by organizing and decluttering our physical surroundings.

Preservation is an individual endeavor and involves cultivating supportive relationships and communities. Surrounding ourselves with positive and like-minded individuals can enhance our ability to preserve our state of mind. Through shared experiences, collaboration, and support, we can sustain our motivation, enthusiasm, and commitment to personal growth and self-improvement.

To truly master the art of preservation, we must also recognize the impermanence of life and embrace change. Flexibility and adaptability are essential qualities that enable us to navigate the challenges and uncertainties that come our way. By acknowledging that change is inevitable and embracing it as an opportunity for growth, we can better preserve our state of mind, even in the face of adversity.

In conclusion, preservation is an integral aspect of the Tantra Learning Framework and involves learning the art of maintaining a state of mind that aligns with one's highest potential. By cultivating self-awareness, practicing meditation and mindfulness, nurturing the body and physical environment, fostering supportive relationships, and embracing change, we can create a solid foundation for personal growth and self-realization. The preservation journey requires commitment, effort, and a deep understanding of ourselves. As we preserve and maintain our state of mind, we unlock the potential to transform our lives and reach new heights of personal and spiritual development.

3. Destruction

In the tantric tradition, destruction is not considered an opposing force but a necessary creation component. Just as the forest floor must be cleared of dead leaves and fallen branches to make way for new growth, we must also embrace the power of destruction to make space for transformation in our lives. Shiva destroys not out of a desire for chaos or destruction but because destruction is necessary for renewal and revival.

For many, the idea of destruction may be unsettling or even terrifying. We may instinctively recoil from the thought of our carefully constructed lives being torn down or demolished. However, the tantric approach invites us to shift our perspective and see destruction as an opportunity for growth and change. As the phoenix rises from the ashes, destruction can lead to renewal and revival.

Destruction is not only necessary but also exciting and entertaining. Just as creation brings joy and awe, so too does destruction. This perspective challenges us to see destruction not as something to be feared but as a dynamic and transformative force. It is a reminder that life is not stagnant but constantly evolving and changing.

4. Forgetting

In pursuing knowledge and growth, it is equally important to recognize the power of forgetting. Our brains can remember almost everything, but they also can quickly forget. In Tantra, forgetting is not seen as a memory failure but rather as a deliberate act of letting go.

The tantra practices teach techniques to make unwanted thoughts and memories disappear as quickly as turning off a switch. This intentional forgetting allows us to release the grip of past experiences and beliefs that no longer serve us. It is a way to clear the slate and create space for new possibilities and growth.

5. Remembering

While forgetting has its place, tantra also recognizes the importance of enhancing memory and the ability to recall information with reliability. Tantra teaches techniques to improve memory at the level of reliability found in computers. We can transcend time and enhance memory by tapping into the power of visualization and imagination.

Through practices such as visualization exercises and mnemonic techniques, tantra allows us to tap into the depths of our minds and access information with unparalleled accuracy. This ability to remember and recall information is a practical skill and a gateway to deeper insights and understanding.

Appendix III: Five Layers of Self

Within Tantra, there is an understanding of the different layers of self and their relationship to reality. When explored and understood, these layers can lead to a more profound sense of self-awareness and a more authentic life experience.

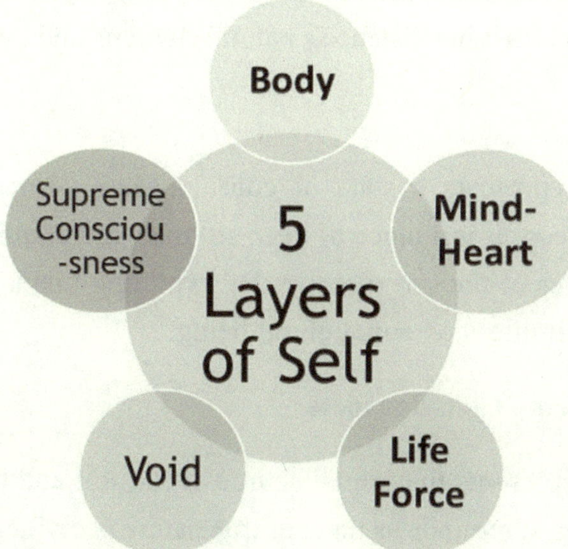

1. The Environment/Body

This layer represents the external environment in which we exist. It includes our physical bodies and the spaces we inhabit. This layer is a reminder that we are interconnected with the world around us and that our well-being is intimately tied to the well-being of our environment.

2. The Mind-Heart

This layer encompasses the thought, action, and emotion continuum. Through this layer, we experience the full spectrum of human experience. It reminds us that our thoughts, actions, and emotions are interconnected and shape our perception of reality.

3. The Life Force

This layer encompasses the bodily systems over which we have little control, such as breathing and digestion. It is a reminder of our mortality and the impermanence of life. This layer invites us to surrender and trust in existence's natural rhythms and cycles.

4. The Void

This layer represents a state of consciousness comparable to a dreamless sleep. It is a place of deep stillness and emptiness where the boundaries of the self dissolve. By exploring this layer, we can tap into the limitless potential of our being.

5. The Supreme Consciousness

This layer represents the primal source of the self and the ultimate state of being. It reminds us that our true nature is divine and that we are interconnected with all existence. This layer invites us to transcend the individual self's limitations and connect with the boundless consciousness that underlies all creation.

In conclusion, this layer of Self offers a profound perspective on the transformative power of destruction, the importance of forgetting and remembering, the exploration of the Veils of Ignorance, and the Powers of God.

Appendix IV: Five Veils of Ignorance (The Intellectual Tattvas)

The five Veils of Ignorance are presented here in a more elaborate form and serve as reinforcement:

Level 7: Action

To truly understand the power and implications of action in Tantra, we must first acknowledge the limitations that come with it. Our desires, fears, and societal constructs often drive our actions. They are necessary for our survival, comfort, and protection. However, these limitations can also shape and confine our perception of reality, sometimes inhibiting our ability to see beyond what is immediately tangible.

Our actions are deeply ingrained in us from a young age. We are taught what is right and wrong, how to behave, and how to navigate societal norms. We learn to move within the limits our families, communities, and the larger society set. Though seemingly necessary, these limitations can restrict our ability to explore and experience the true essence of Tantra.

By understanding the limitations imposed by our actions, we can begin to challenge and transcend them. Tantra offers a path that encourages us to go beyond the confines of our conditioned actions. It invites us to explore the depths of our desires, fears, and emotions and uncover the conditioning layers that shape our perception of reality.

Through the practice of Tantra, we learn to become aware of the unconscious patterns that govern our actions. We are encouraged to question our motivations and intentions to uncover the underlying beliefs and fears that guide our decisions. By doing so, we can begin to recognize the limitations our actions impose on us and consciously work towards expanding our perception of reality.

This expanded perception of reality can greatly inform instructional design in Tantra learning. Educators must go beyond traditional teaching methods bound by societal norms and expectations. We must create a learning environment that encourages exploration, self-expression, and a deep understanding of the self.

Incorporating Tantra principles into instructional design allows for a more holistic approach to learning. It calls for recognizing the learner's physical, emotional, and spiritual interconnectedness. By creating a safe space for learners to explore their limitations, fears, and desires, we empower them to transcend the boundaries set by their actions and expand their perception of reality.

In Tantra learning, action is not simply a means to an end but a gateway to self-discovery and transformation. Through conscious action, we can uncover truths about ourselves and the world around us that were previously hidden. We can break free from the limitations imposed by societal conditioning and embrace a more authentic and expansive perception of reality.

As I continue my exploration of Tantra learning and instructional design, I am reminded of the immense power that lies within our actions. They can shape our perception of reality and transform our lives in ways we never thought possible. By understanding and exploring the limitations of our actions, we can unlock a world of possibilities and create a learning framework that is profoundly transformative, empowering, and rooted in the essence of Tantra.

Level 8: Knowledge

In traditional instructional design, knowledge is often considered an end-point, the final destination in the learning journey. Learners are expected to acquire knowledge and reproduce it accurately. However, Tantra invites us to view knowledge as a dynamic force that cannot be fully grasped but can be experienced and felt.

One of the fundamental principles of Tantra is recognizing that knowledge is limited. No matter how well-versed we are in a particular subject or how many facts we gather, there will always be something beyond our grasp. Tantra discourages the illusion of absolute knowledge, urging us to embrace the constant curiosity and wonder that accompanies the pursuit of knowledge.

In Tantra's realm, the power of knowledge lies not in acquiring a vast amount of information but in developing the ability to distinguish between beliefs, facts, and lies. It encourages us to question the foundation on which our knowledge is built and to challenge our assumptions. Tantra invites us to examine how our knowledge may be influenced by societal norms, cultural biases, and personal experiences, thus deepening our understanding of ourselves and the world around us.

Self-expression, a vital aspect of Tantra, is an act of creation, renovation, and evolution. Through self-expression, one can voice thoughts, emotions, and experiences that would otherwise remain hidden. As we engage in self-expression, we generate new knowledge by articulating our ideas and the insights and revelations that emerge from the act.

Preservation of knowledge holds excellent significance in Tantra. Just as a seed needs to be nurtured and protected to grow into a fully bloomed flower, knowledge requires preservation to maintain its potency. Tantra teaches us to value the wisdom passed down through generations, recognizing the importance of preserving the knowledge that forms the foundation of our understanding.

However, Tantra also emphasizes the necessity of destruction for renewal and revival. Just as a forest fire rages through the old, decaying vegetation, clearing the way for new growth, the destruction of existing knowledge paves the path for fresh perspectives and insights. Tantra teaches us that clinging to outdated ideas and beliefs impedes our growth, and it is only through the release of old notions that we can make space for transformative learning experiences.

Knowledge, therefore, is not a static destination but a journey of constant exploration and discovery. Tantra provides a framework that guides us through this journey, reminding us to abandon the confines of certainty and embrace the vastness of the unknown. In the realm of instructional design, this understanding prompts a shift in focus from knowledge acquisition to cultivating a mindset of lifelong learning. It encourages creating learning experiences that ignite curiosity, fosters critical thinking, and nurture a sense of wonder.

By embracing the inherent limitations of knowledge and surrendering to the constant quest for deeper understanding, we can genuinely transform the instructional design and unlock the transformative potential of Tantra in education.

Level 9: Desire

To understand the significance of desire in the learning process, we must first acknowledge its fundamental role in human motivation. Desire, by definition, is an intense longing or craving for something. This longing can be directed toward various aspects of life, such as knowledge, success, or self-expression. It is pivotal in driving individuals towards achieving their goals, fueling the inherent curiosity and ambition that propel us forward.

In instructional design, desires can be powerful catalysts for personal growth and transformation. Learners become actively engaged in learning When they are motivated by their desires. They pursue knowledge with passion and enthusiasm, going beyond the mere acquisition of information to embrace a deeper understanding of the subject matter. This intrinsic motivation stemming from desire creates a fertile ground for transformative educational experiences.

Unfortunately, societal norms often discourage indulgence in desires, particularly within educational contexts. There is a prevailing belief that desires distract us from pursuing academic excellence, leading us astray from the prescribed path of knowledge. We are conditioned to curtail our desires, to view them as obstacles rather than growth opportunities. This perspective limits our potential for exploration and diminishes the transformative power of education.

However, it is essential to challenge these societal norms and prioritize desire-based learning experiences. Embracing desire allows learners to cultivate a sense of agency and autonomy in their educational journey. Acknowledging their desires, they take ownership of their learning, pursuing topics and approaches that resonate with their passions and interests. This personal connection to the material enhances motivation and fosters a deep and lasting engagement with the subject matter.

A desire-based instructional design framework encourages educators to design learning experiences that tap into learners' passions and aspirations. It requires a shift from a standardized, one-size-fits-all approach to one that acknowledges the uniqueness of each individual. Through personalized learning paths and tailored experiences, learners are empowered to explore their desires within education.

Incorporating desire-based learning experiences in instructional design frameworks enriches the educational journey and promotes holistic personal growth and transformation. Learners are exposed to various emotions and experiences when they engage with their desires. They learn to navigate challenges, persevere through obstacles, and acquire the skills necessary to manifest their desires into reality.

Moreover, desire-based learning experiences encourage learners to think critically and creatively. As they delve deep into their passions, they develop the capacity for innovation, problem-solving, and effective decision-making. By fostering an environment that values desires and celebrates individuality, instructional design frameworks can cultivate knowledgeable, well-rounded, and self-aware learners.

To fully embrace desire in education, we must create a space that encourages vulnerability and authenticity. Learners should feel safe and supported in expressing their desires without fear of judgment or ridicule. We can create an environment that fosters growth and empowerment by challenging societal norms that discourage indulgence in desires. We can pave the way for a truly transformative educational experience through open-mindedness and compassion.

In conclusion, desire is a potent force that has the potential to revolutionize instructional design. By emphasizing its importance in learning, we challenge societal norms and empower learners to explore their passions and aspirations. Incorporating desire-based learning experiences in instructional design frameworks enhances motivation and engagement and facilitates personal growth and transformation. Learners become active agents in their education when desires are embraced, fostering creativity, critical thinking, and self-awareness. Let us cast aside the constraints of societal norms and unleash the transformative power of desire in education.

Level 10: Time

Time is a mysterious and elusive concept that has fascinated philosophers, scientists, and spiritual seekers for centuries. It holds a powerful grip on our lives, dictating our schedules, organizing our daily activities, and shaping our world perception. Yet, despite its undeniable presence and influence, time remains a profoundly enigmatic force, often defying our attempts to grasp its essence.

In the realm of Tantra, time takes on an entirely different meaning. Tantra challenges the linear perception of time, inviting us to question its boundaries and explore the possibilities of transcending its limitations. It urges us to delve into the depths of our consciousness and tap into the timeless essence that lies within.

The concept of time in Tantra goes beyond the traditional understanding of a linear progression from past to future. Instead, it is a dynamic and fluid energy that can be harnessed to create transformative experiences. Tantra recognizes that time is not solely confined to the external realm but also resides within us, intimately woven into the fabric of our existence. It is an integral part of our consciousness, influencing our thoughts, emotions, and actions.

One of the ways Tantra allows us to engage with time is through imaginative visualization. In Tantric practices, visualizations serve as powerful tools for recreating experiences from the past, thus breaking the linear constraints of time. By vividly imagining ourselves in a particular moment, we can tap into its energy and essence, transcending the boundaries of the present moment. Through this process, we gain a deeper understanding of our past experiences and can use them to inform and shape our present and future.

Tantra invites us to explore the limitations of time and discover how we can transcend them through various practices. Meditation, for example, is a powerful tool that enables us to go beyond the constraints of time and enter a timeless state of awareness. As we sit in stillness, our minds become attuned to the present moment, transcending the constant stream of thoughts and worries that often dominate our consciousness. Time loses its hold on us in this state, and we can tap into a deeper, more expansive awareness.

Similarly, visualization techniques play a significant role in transcending time limitations. By vividly picturing a desired outcome or experience, we can create a bridge between the present and the future, collapsing the distance between them. Through the power of our imagination, we can manifest our intentions, shaping our reality in ways that defy the linear perception of time. Tantra teaches us that time constraints do not bind us; we can shape and mold it to align with our desires and aspirations.

The limitations of time, as perceived by the linear mind, are mere illusions in the realm of Tantra. Time's forward movement can be transcended, and its constraints can be broken through conscious engagement with our inner selves. Tantra offers us the tools and practices to explore the dimensions of time, recognizing that it is not merely an external force but an integral aspect of our being.

In this exploration, we discover that time is not a fixed entity but a malleable energy that can be harnessed and manipulated. We realize that our perception of time is not an objective truth but a subjective experience shaped by our consciousness. By expanding our awareness and engaging with our innermost being, we unravel the conditioning and limitations that restrict our relationship with time. We learn to embrace the fluidity of time and dance with its rhythms, finding grace and ease in the ever-changing flow.

Tantra teaches us that time is not something to be conquered or overcome but rather an ally to be befriended and understood. It invites us to let go of our attachment to a linear perception of time and embrace the vastness of the present moment. In this expansiveness, we find liberation from the constraints of past and future, and we can fully embody the timeless essence that resides within us.

As we immerse ourselves in the teachings and practices of Tantra, we begin to unravel the layers of conditioning that have confined us to a limited perception of time. We open ourselves to the infinite possibilities beyond the confines of the linear mind, expanding our consciousness to encompass the timeless realm. In this spaciousness, we come alive and awaken to the fullness of our being, liberated from the shackles of time.

Tantra invites us to embark on a journey of exploration and discovery, unraveling the mysteries of time and transcending its limitations. Through meditation, visualization, and conscious engagement with our inner selves, we can tap into the timeless essence that resides within and align ourselves with the natural rhythms of the universe. In this alignment, we find harmony and balance, embracing the ever-changing dance of time and its boundless potential.

Embracing the teachings of Tantra, we transcend the linear perception of time and step into a realm of infinite possibilities. We become architects of our destiny, shaping time to align with our deepest desires and aspirations. In this dance with time, we discover the power and beauty of our existence, embracing the fullness of the present moment and the timeless essence that lies within us all.

Level 11: Cause and Effect

As an avid researcher and practitioner of the Tantra learning framework, I have come to reevaluate the notion of cause and effect and its profound impact on our understanding of reality and karma. Tantra teaches that cause and effect is one of the Veils of Ignorance that obscures our perception of the true nature of existence. To truly grasp the depths of the Tattvas and their transformative potential in instructional design, we must first shed the limiting belief in the simplistic cause-and-effect relationship.

Most conventional educational systems and instructional designs assume a linear relationship exists between cause and effect. According to this view, an action performed by an individual will inevitably lead to a corresponding consequence. While this understanding may seem practical and logical on the surface, Tantra challenges us to delve deeper into the intricacies of reality.

In Tantra, cause and effect are seen as a superficial understanding of the dynamic interplay of energy and consciousness. It is believed that the deterministic view of cause and effect fails to account for the complexities and interconnectedness of the universe. Rather than a linear progression of events, Tantra unveils a multidimensional web of interdependent factors, where every action and experience is intertwined with the totality of existence.

When we reevaluate the notion of cause and effect through the lens of Tantra, we begin to perceive a more holistic perspective on reality and karma. Tantra teaches that everything in the universe is interrelated, and each action reverberates through the interconnected web of existence. This understanding challenges the simplistic idea that a single cause will inevitably lead to a predictable effect. Instead, Tantra suggests that every cause contributes to many effects, each rippling through the fabric of reality in unique and unpredictable ways.

By embracing this expanded understanding of cause and effect, instructional design can be transformed within the Tantra learning framework. Traditional instructional designs often focus on isolated cause-and-effect relationships, aiming to produce specific outcomes through predetermined methods. However, when we acknowledge the interconnectedness of all things, we realize that rigid instructional designs may limit the potential for profound transformation and growth.

In the Tantra learning framework, instructional design becomes a dynamic and organic process shaped by the interplay of energies and consciousness. Rather than imposing a fixed set of methods and outcome expectations, the Tantra approach invites a co-creative engagement between the teacher, the learner, and the inherent intelligence of the universe. Instructional design becomes a dance of intuition, responsiveness, and adaptability.

Through this re-evaluation of cause and effect, instructional design can transcend the limitations of rigid methodologies and predetermined outcomes. Instead of seeking to control and manipulate the learning process, Tantra invites educators to surrender to the wisdom of the Tattvas and the flow of energy. Instructional design becomes the art of creating a supportive and empowering environment where learners are encouraged to explore their unique paths of growth and self-discovery.

Within the Tantra learning framework, the re-evaluation of cause and effect also extends to our understanding of karma. Karma, often misinterpreted as a mechanical system of retribution and reward, is seen through the lens of Tantra as a dynamic and interrelated web of energetic imprints. Rather than a linear cause-and-effect relationship, Tantra reveals karma as a complex intertwining of actions, intentions, and energetic consequences that shape our experiences.

By re-evaluating the notion of cause and effect and its impact on our understanding of reality and karma, we open ourselves to a deeper exploration of the transformative potential of the Tattvas in instructional design. The Tantra learning framework invites us to embrace the complexity and interdependence of existence, freeing ourselves from the limitations of linear thinking.

In conclusion, cause and effect is a Veil of Ignorance that obscures our perception of the true nature of reality. Tantra challenges us to go beyond simplistic notions of cause and effect and embrace a more holistic understanding of the interconnectedness of all things. This re-evaluation of cause and effect can transform instructional design within the Tantra learning framework, allowing for a more dynamic and co-creative approach that honors the uniqueness of each learner's path. By recognizing the multidimensionality of cause and effect and the intricacy of karma, we can unlock the transformative potential of the Tattvas in educational settings, paving the way for profound growth and self-realization.

Appendix V: The 6 Occult Tattvas

Levels 6 to 0 Maya, Wisdom, God, Beyond God, Shakti, Shiva, The Secret Tattva

(This Appendix completes the list of the 36 Tattvas.)

Tantric Occult Science explores Tantra in the modern context. However, to understand the unique attributes of Tantric Occultism, we must first understand Occultism itself. Occultism is the domain of human consciousness that one cannot express in words. Every human being has emotions that are similar but not identical. (*Refer to the section on Qualia.*) In this context, Occult experiences are not daily occurrences.

6. Maya

Maya is an illusion, and illusion is everything! Therefore, everything is Maya! In Tantric Occult Science, these statements are genuine. Remember that we are questioning 'Reality' and challenging the popular idea of 'Reality.' We need to interpret "illusion" as "illumination." Light falls on an object, and we can see it – that is Maya. Neurons fire and thoughts emerge in the brain: that too is Maya.

Maya is everything that manifests itself either as an object or as a thought. The power of appearance (thing or idea) is Maya. Maya is imagination in its totality: from the 'image' of an object the eye creates in the brain to fantasies to conjuring thoughts.

5. Wisdom

This is wisdom in its classical sense: a vibration every creature possesses. A smell, a sound, a rhythm, a color… anything that "vibrates" within us and connects us to our environment purely through non-verbal means is wisdom. The wind is blowing, and the trees are swaying in its flow. The wind is also rustling my hair as if they are leaves. It is raising the dust and the pollen and making crows and butterflies dance in the air: this is wisdom.

Wisdom is the non-verbal realization arising out of our minds' framework. It is not smartness but an innate form of consciousness that everyone is born with.

4. God

This is the standard concept of God. Tantra states that everyone has a personal deity (call it what you may or may not name it), which is the level on which we place all known gods. This level of consciousness does not separate itself from anything else. This consciousness sees itself in everything (omnipresence) and can identify the other as itself.

"I am that I am!"

God is each individual's personal and private affair, so there are as many gods as the people with a belief system. Even if you believe in 'One God,' your idea of that one god is always unique. Therefore, Tantra states that there are many gods, even if you call them by one name or many names or prefer not to name them at all!

This level is not the prerogative of some unknown (or unknowable) supernatural being – anyone can attain it. It is also unsurprising to see cats, snakes, and other animals worshiped as gods. In animism, nature and animals gain the stature of a god. Thus, you can be God and then go beyond God!

3. Beyond God

The formative principles of a fully expanded mind will naturally lead to realizing a consciousness beyond the ultimate. When tantriks attain the God level, it soon bores them. They will create – or become the causative agent – for an idea that exceeds God.

Level 2 and Level 1: Shakti and Shiva

Shakti and Shiva are not deities as popularly worshiped. Tantric Occult Science states that deep levels of consciousness exist simultaneously but are experienced sequentially. Shakti is the creative force: we experience Shakti as the constant flow of thoughts, and Shiva is the space of stillness between the views. Shiva is subtle, and Shakti is apparent.

One attains Shakti, but one can only achieve Shiva. The feminine and masculine forms are for linguistic convenience and make no difference to the ideas of Shiva and Shakti. Any association with feminine and masculine virtues is inconsequential. One could call Shakti masculine and Shiva feminine, which would make no difference in Tantra. (Some schools of Tantra consider Shiva feminine and Shakti masculine.)

You can experience Shakti and Shiva by practicing some Pranayama (breathing exercises). The inhaling and exhaling are Shakti, and holding your breath between these acts is Shiva. In meditation, it is the experience of stillness between the flows of thoughts: the silence of time between one thought leaving and another entering.

There are many techniques to experience these levels of consciousness, but Shiva and Shakti are not explainable or describable – you have to "feel" them. Consider this exercise from a Buddhist practice: take a sip of water and hold it in your mouth. Do not fill your mouth. Now, depending on how you expand or contract your cheeks, you will "feel" your mouth full of water or air.

Similarly, when doing Pranayam, instead of focusing on the air coming in and going out of your lungs, focus on the emptiness of the lungs filling up (while inhaling) and then the lungs becoming empty again (while exhaling). The breathing exercise has not changed, but your mind now focuses on the emptiness rather than the air coming and going.

Another example: We enjoy a full stomach, especially when the food is good, but try enjoying an empty stomach. I am not talking about starving, but simple fasting: the experience of the space within our body can be pretty exciting. This emptiness is Shiva!

Level 0: The Secret Tattva

This tattva is a secret because one tantrik's experience of it differs from that of another tantrik. This is at the highest level of tattvas because it encompasses all the other tattvas, including Shakti and Shiva. It is the level of the pure Occult – no words can describe the experience. Words will be a waste of paper, and reading those words will be a waste of time.

Essentially, this is a secret not because we keep it that way but because my experience is unique, indescribable, and incomprehensible to another Yogi.

www.ingramcontent.com/pod-product-compliance
Lightning Source LLC
LaVergne TN
LVHW041036150826
845672LV00001B/345

* 9 7 9 8 8 9 2 7 7 8 4 1 1 *